SHAPING A
PROFESSIONAL IDENTITY

Stories of Educational Practice

SHAPING A PROFESSIONAL IDENTITY

Stories of Educational Practice

F. MICHAEL CONNELLY
D. JEAN CLANDININ
EDITORS

—WITH—

SHEILA DERMER APPLEBAUM   JANICE HUBER
NORMAN BEACH   JOANN PHILLION
CHERYL CRAIG   SALLY QUAN
ANNIE DAVIES   CHUCK ROSE
JINJIANG DU   FLORENCE SAMSON
MING FANG HE   KAREN WHELAN

TEACHERS
COLLEGE
PRESS

TEACHERS COLLEGE
COLUMBIA UNIVERSITY
NEW YORK AND LONDON

Published by Teachers College Press, 1234 Amsterdam Avenue, New York, NY 10027

Library of Congress Cataloging-in-Publication Data

Shaping a professional identity: Stories of educational practice / F. Michael Connelly,
   D. Jean Clandinin, editors.
      p.   cm.
   Includes bibliographical references (p.   ) and index.
   ISBN 0-8077-3849-2 (cloth). — ISBN 0-8077-3848-4 (paper)
      1. Education—Biographical methods.   2. Teachers—Attitudes.
   3. School administrators—Attitudes.   4. Teaching—Case studies.
   5. School management and organization—Case studies.   6. Knowledge,
   Theory of.   I. Connelly, F. Michael.   II. Clandinin, D. Jean.
   LB1029.B55S86   1999
   371.1—dc21   98-56525

ISBN 0-8077-3848-4 (paper)
ISBN 0-8077-3849-2 (cloth)

Printed on acid-free paper
Manufactured in the United States of America

06 05 04 03 02 01 00 99   8 7 6 5 4 3 2 1

Contents

Acknowledgments

This book comes out of a 20-year collaboration into questions of teacher knowledge. Over these years we have worked with many graduate students, teachers, and student teachers. Without our continued conversations with them, both in and out of their schools and classrooms, the understandings that are part of this book would not have been possible. It is from living these conversations, and from our reflections on these conversations, that we have come to understand something of the interconnectedness of knowledge, context, and identity.

We owe a particular debt to the authors, and their participants, for telling and retelling their stories with us and for responding to our stories. Finally, our thanks to Gary Pyper for continuing to find ways to facilitate the many iterations of this text, much of it electronically, across the Canadian expanse.

The Social Science and Humanities Research Council of Canada has been a long-term and constant supporter of our research.

CHAPTER 1

Knowledge, Context, and Identity

We have been students of teacher knowledge for many years. When we began this line of work in the 1970s, the field of teacher thinking was just emerging in the educational research literature. Prior to that, researchers focused on teacher skills, attitudes, characteristics, and methods. There was excitement throughout the research community when attention turned to teachers' thought processes. It was felt by many that this was a move closer to the experience of classrooms, a move that would bring life to the field. Even then, however, there was little talk of teachers as holders and makers of knowledge. For example, in the third edition of the *Handbook of Research on Teaching* (Wittrock, 1986), the only references to teacher knowledge research were comparatively minor citations in two chapters titled "Teachers' Thought Processes" (Clark & Peterson, 1986) and "The Cultures of Teaching" (Feiman-Nemser & Floden, 1986).

Following the work of Dewey (1938), Schwab (1970), Polanyi (1958), Gauthier (1963), Johnson (1987), and others, we became fascinated with trying to understand teachers as knowers: knowers of themselves, of their situations, of children, of subject matter, of teaching, of learning. To reflect our epistemological interest in the personal and practical nature of education we coined the term "personal practical knowledge," which we defined as the following:

> A term designed to capture the idea of experience in a way that allows us to talk about teachers as knowledgeable and knowing persons. Personal practical knowledge is in the teacher's past experience, in the teacher's present mind and body, and in the future plans and actions. Personal practical knowledge is found in the teacher's practice. It is, for any teacher, a particular way of reconstructing the past and the intentions of the future to deal with the exigencies of a present situation. (Connelly & Clandinin, 1988, p. 25)

Increasingly, as our work progressed, we came to see teacher knowledge in terms of narrative life history, as storied life compositions. These stories, these narratives of experience, are both personal—reflecting a person's life history—and social—reflecting the milieu, the contexts in which teachers live. Keeping our eyes firmly on the question of teacher knowledge, we realized that knowledge was both formed and expressed in context. Within schools this context is immensely complex and we adopted a metaphor of a professional knowledge landscape to help us capture this complexity.

> A landscape metaphor is particularly well suited to our purpose. It allows us to talk about space, place, and time. Furthermore, it has a sense of expansiveness and the possibility of being filled with diverse people, things, and events in different relationships. Understanding professional knowledge as comprising a landscape calls for a notion of professional knowledge as composed of a wide variety of components and influenced by a wide variety of people, places, and things. Because we see the professional knowledge landscape as composed of relationships among people, places, and things, we see it as both an intellectual and a moral landscape. (Clandinin & Connelly, 1995, pp 4–5)

We view the landscape as narratively constructed: as having a history with moral, emotional, and aesthetic dimensions. We see it as storied. To enter a professional knowledge landscape is to enter a place of story. The landscape is composed of two fundamentally different places, the in-classroom place and the out-of-classroom place. We described the out-of-classroom place as:

> a place filled with knowledge funneled into the school system for the purpose of altering teachers' and children's classroom lives. Teachers talk about this knowledge all the time. We all make reference to "what's coming down the pipe"; "what's coming down now"; "what will they throw down on us next". In these metaphorical expressions we hear teachers express their knowledge of their out-of-classroom place as a place littered with imposed prescriptions. It is a place filled with other people's visions of what is right for children. Researchers, policy makers, senior administrators and others, using various implementation strategies, push research findings, policy statements, plans, improvement schemes and so on down what we call the conduit into this out-of-classroom place on the professional knowledge landscape. We characterize this theory-driven view of practice shared by practitioners, policy makers, and theoreticians as having the quality of what Crites (1971) called a sacred story.

With respect to the in-classroom place we wrote:

> Classrooms are, for the most part, safe places, generally free from scrutiny, where teachers are free to live stories of practice. These lived stories are essentially

secret ones. Furthermore, when these secret lived stories are told, they are, for the most part, told to other teachers in other secret places. When teachers move out of their classrooms onto the out-of-classroom place on the landscape, they often live and tell cover stories, stories in which they portray themselves as experts, certain characters whose teacher stories fit within the acceptable range of the story of school being lived in the school. Cover stories enable teachers whose teacher stories are marginalized by whatever the current story of school is to continue to practice and to sustain their teacher stories. (Clandinin & Connelly, 1996, p. 25)

Soltis (1995) summarized our language of the landscape as a "language of 'secret places,' 'sacred stories,' 'cover stories,' the 'conduit,' and its 'rhetoric of conclusions'—categories designed to penetrate our social construction of the reality of teaching and schooling" (p. vii). In addition to our recognizing the secret, sacred, and cover stories that make up the landscape, we realized that stories were also told about people and about institutions. We came to differentiate these as teacher stories and stories of teachers, school stories and stories of schools. This latter set of stories might, depending on the circumstances, be secret stories or cover stories. Sacred stories have a special quality.

We developed the notions of personal practical knowledge and professional knowledge landscape, both narrative educational concepts, as a way of understanding teacher knowledge. They are key terms in our way of speaking about teacher knowledge. Teachers and others who work in schools resonated with this language. They welcomed us into their classrooms, responded positively in ours, engaged in collaborative enquiries with us, and so on. By their responses we were encouraged to continue framing our questions in terms of knowledge. However, we began to sense subtle differences. We noticed that teachers seemed to be trying to answer different questions. Their questions were ones of identity. They were questions of "Who am I in my story of teaching?"; "Who am I in my place in the school?"; "Who am I in children's stories?"; "Who am I in my administrator's stories?"; "Who am I in parents' stories?" and so on. We began to listen more closely. What we heard intrigued us. In graduate student writing, in teacher inquiry groups, and in research meetings, teachers were more inclined to ask questions along the lines of "Who am I in this situation?" than "What do I know in this situation?" Teachers seemed more concerned to ask questions of who they are than of what they know.

The puzzle for us, and the puzzle we pursue in this book, is the connectedness between teachers' questions of identity and our own of teacher knowledge. Our sense as we began our project on which this book is based is that teachers' concerns and our own were intricately related. But how? We knew that our language of narrative and story was the connection that allowed us, with comparative ease, to negotiate working relationships with teachers, to talk with them on a collegial basis, and to pursue teaching-learning relationships with them. Our puzzle, then, was that we sensed that teachers could use our work to get answers to their questions and to figure out who they were, yet in doing so, they were answering different questions from those with which we began.

As we listened to practitioners and conducted the work on which this book is based, we realized that the theoretical puzzle was to link knowledge, context, and identity. We developed a further term to begin to make this link, namely, "stories to live by." This term is the intellectual thread that holds this book together. This thread helps us to understand how knowledge, context, and identity are linked and can be understood narratively.

Stories to live by, the phrase used throughout this book to refer to identity, is given meaning by the narrative understandings of knowledge and context. Stories to live by are shaped by such matters as secret teacher stories, sacred stories of schooling, and teachers' cover stories.

In research groups, teachers and administrators told, listened, and responded to each others' stories and came to represent these conversations in individually authored chapters. Our own writing in what follows is metalevel writing, texts constructed as we read and interpreted our colleagues' accounts. This approach gives the book a particular structure of accounts of practice in Parts I and III and our reflections on those accounts in Parts II and IV. Not only did we engage in many of the conversations that led up to the individually authored chapters, we read and reread those chapters searching for practitioner ways of speaking about what mattered to them in their stories to live by. We had no preset agenda or intellectual framework other than our interest in the interconnectedness of knowledge, context, and identity. What emerged were chapters that dealt with the links between identity and curriculum making; the ways in which identities are composed, sustained, and changed; the links between borders of space, time, and identity; and preliminary notions of the connections between identity and hierarchies of authority. As we continue to read and reread these chapters we may see as yet unexplored themes and connections linking practitioner knowledge, context, and identity. Readers, too, may do this.

It turned out to be important to the book that each of us had a sabbatical during the writing. At first we imagined that the sabbaticals would make more time available for writing. They did, but they did more than this. By stepping out of the dailiness of our work lives at the same time as we were reading and thinking about the work lives of our colleagues, we became more aware of the passing of time. We experienced a sense of temporality about schooling not readily seen in the studies and experiences reported in Parts I and III. We had a sense of changing landscapes over long periods of time and conclude Part II with an essay on temporality and identity. We end Part IV with reflections on administrators' stories to live by.

Note: Throughout this book, pseudonyms are used for all people mentioned, except for the chapter authors.

PART I

Teacher Stories, Stories of Teachers, School Stories, Stories of School

Part I is composed of chapters in which teachers tell their own stories and of chapters in which researchers tell stories of teachers. In one chapter a teacher story is written by researchers and the teacher whose story is told. In all of the chapters the stories are situated on both the in- and out-of-classroom places. Because there were so many ongoing conversations among ourselves and the authors of these chapters, we developed, together, the ideas and terms described in Chapter 1. These ideas and terms, then, both helped shape the chapters that follow and were in our minds as we read them in preparation for writing Part II. Some of the key terms in Part I are *professional knowledge landscape, in-classroom place, out-of-classroom place, sacred story of theory-driven practice, conduit, cover story,* and *story to live by.* Woven throughout are the ideas of teacher stories, stories of teachers, school stories, and stories of school. The reader will not find simple one-to-one applications of these terms and ideas in the stories. The terms and ideas weave in and out in complex ways depending on the story and its context.

CHAPTER 2

Listening to Children
on the Landscape

Janice Huber

"No, I didn't!"

"Yes, you did!"

"I took the ball outside, it was mine. I didn't say you could play with it,
did I, huh? Huh?"

"Lance said I could play."

"I got the ball first today so I was the boss of the ball and I didn't say
you could play. Lance is a loser, he always plays with you. What's
he? Your boooyfriennnnnd? Anyways, what Lance says doesn't
matter. Oh crybaby, what're you going to teeeell? Go ahead, see if
I care. You're such a loser!"

This was the angry interchange that echoed down the hallway and around
the corner as Shaun, my junior teaching partner, and I left the staff room on a
late fall afternoon and walked toward the assigned entrance where we greeted
our children each morning and afternoon. As we turned the corner and
began to walk the last distance to meet them, two of our children, Ameel
and Monica, rounded the corner at the far end of the hallway, yelling and
pushing each other. These were the two children to whom the loud, shouting, angry voices belonged.

Shaun continued to the entrance to meet the remainder of our class while
I stopped to talk with Ameel and Monica. As their voices continued to esca-
late, they appeared not to notice that I was present. In a voice much louder
than I was accustomed to using, I told them to stop and sit down on one of
the small benches outside our classroom where the children's mailboxes were
placed. Setting the mailboxes on the floor and motioning for the children to

Shaping a Professional Identity: Stories of Educational Practice. Copyright © 1999 by Teachers College, Columbia University. All
rights reserved. ISBN 0-8077-3848-4 (pbk.), ISBN 0-8077-3849-2 (cloth). Prior to photocopying items for classroom use, please
contact the Copyright Clearance Center, Customer Service, 222 Rosewood Dr., Danvers, MA 01923, USA, tel. (508) 750-8400.

join me, I sat down. Ameel and Monica sat, one on either side of me. I asked what had happened. They explained that they were arguing about a ball they had been playing with outside. Earlier in the fall, the children in our classroom had decided that whenever they felt angry, upset, or frustrated with one another, they would sit down together and talk about their concerns until they felt they had made further sense of them. When they felt as though they had been as thoughtful as possible about their concerns, either Shaun or I invited the children to discuss what they had figured out. I asked Monica and Ameel if they would like to remain on the bench for a few minutes to discuss their concerns before coming to talk about them with Shaun or me. They agreed. Leaving them to their conversation, I proceeded into the classroom where the remainder of our children were scattered throughout the room, reading in groups, pairs, or independently.

Within a few minutes, angry, raised voices echoed back into the classroom. When I walked into the hallway, Monica and Ameel were standing nose to nose, each with their hands on their hips, screaming at each other. Although I had already seen angry exchanges between the children within this grouping earlier during the fall, these situations had not contained the same degree of anger I was currently witnessing between these two children. After separating them and once again, seating myself between them, I asked each child to tell me his or her side of the story. When it was Ameel's turn to talk, he immediately started shouting, his voice growing louder and louder as he continued to speak. I finally stopped him and asked, "Why are you shouting at me?" His dark eyes simmered as he looked at me and yelled, "Because I'm mad!"

Contextualizing Our Place on the Landscape

I have shared this story as a beginning way to explore the in-classroom place on the professional knowledge landscape of schools. The context of both the story shared above, and the ongoing narrative, is within a Year 1 and 2 classroom shaped by Shaun, a student teacher for 2 years, the 22 children in our care, and myself.

As the school year in which this story is situated drew near, Shaun and I focused on the in-classroom place. When the children entered into this space we wanted it to feel warm and inviting, creating for them a feeling that it would be an exciting and happy place in which to live for the upcoming year. We covered the bulletin boards with colorful paper and borders, arranged the furniture so that the room felt open and inviting yet also included some quiet "by-myself places." We hung messages such as "a friend is someone with whom you dare to be yourself" (Bergsma, 1983); "We are all the colors of the rainbow" (Landry, 1976); and "I am special and unique." We draped a large, colorful Chinese kite from the ceiling. We organized materials for a variety of center areas, including puppets, listening, friendship, creating, writing, painting, and math. We scattered an assortment of small carpets throughout the room to give our in-classroom place a warm, somewhat cozy feeling.

The first day of school finally arrived, and with a great deal of anticipation, we met our 22 children for the first time. Our beginning work with these children focused on the personal gifts each child brought from his or her life to our classroom community and how these gifts helped to shape our in-classroom place. By imagining our in-classroom place around the metaphor of a garden, we wanted to highlight the individuality of each child and help them to see his or her place and responsibility as a gardener within our community.

We drew upon a vast collection of literature to enrich our classroom experiences. For example, we asked the children to reflect on a poem describing the gentle ripples shaped by a pebble as it was dropped into a pond. As we discussed the life space of this pond community, the children began to imagine what kind of "ripples" they would make within our classroom community. We read *The Salamander Room* (Mazer, 1991) and asked the children to work on collaborative writing and artwork illustrating what kind of "place" our classroom community could be. We read *Crow Boy* (Yashima, 1955) and had the children write and talk about their own personal gifts. We used the story of *Swimmy* (Lionni, 1963) to help us think about what our classroom creed might be. From this story, the children developed the motto: When people love, they bring love to life.

Stories and activities such as these shaped our work during the months of September and October. Before long our in-classroom space became alive. Pieces of writing, a variety of artwork, and photographs of the children were hung throughout the room, in the entrance, and in the hallway outside the classroom. During class time, the children worked at groups of desks or in small clusters throughout the room, and often we gathered together on the carpet in a corner of the room that we called the "cozy corner." Throughout the moments of each day, children's voices filled the room, sometimes quietly, sometimes loudly. At recess, it was not unusual to see the children skipping out of the classroom and down the hallway, hand in hand.

Each morning we gathered in the communal space of our "support circle" to listen to and give response to one another's writing. The children loved this time and were as eager to share their writing as they were to offer response. The making of our support circle had been an especially memorable event early in the school year. We introduced the idea of making a support circle to the children by reading *The Rag Coat* (Mills, 1991), which tells the story of Minna, a young girl who wants to go to school but cannot because she lacks a winter coat. The Quilting Mothers, who gather at Minna's house to make quilts with her mother, offer to make Minna a winter coat from the scraps of fabric left over from their quilting. The Quilting Mothers explain to Minna that each fabric scrap tells a story about the people to whom the fabric belonged.

After reading the story we drew the children into conversation. The children talked about Minna's rag coat and how special it was because it was made of many different pieces of fabric. They discussed the sadness they felt when Minna's classmates laughed at her coat, and they told stories of people they knew who quilted. Threads of the garden metaphor, mentioned earlier, wove into our conversation as we talked about diversity and difference and how something is even more beautiful when colors are mixed, as in a rainbow. We talked about how our classroom was like Minna's coat because all of the children were different, yet we lived together in one room. We asked the children if they would like to make a special kind of classroom quilt so that we would always have a symbol of how important being different yet working together is. The children eagerly agreed and scattered throughout the classroom to design their own piece of the quilt. When all of the children had completed their pieces, made of paper, we talked about how these were like a puzzle, fitting together into the shape of a large circle. After we glued the pieces together, we asked the children to move into the cozy corner, and to sit in a large circle. They immediately saw the connection we were making between how we were sitting and our paper circle. We talked about how we hoped we could meet in a support circle each day to listen to and to respond to the stories we were composing. We asked the children to describe what kind of place they imagined the support circle might be. Using words such as "caring," "helping," and "encouraging," the children explained the kind of place they imagined. Throughout the fall, we enjoyed many special moments in the support circle as the children read their stories and their classmates, Shaun, or I responded to their writing.

Surface Stories of the Landscape

From the outside it likely appeared as though the children, Shaun, and I had developed a deep sense of caring and trust for all individuals within our classroom. A surface telling, such as this, could leave you with the impression that our intentions of building a caring classroom community had been both successful and uneventful. In fact, it was not long before we found ourselves living the dilemma of having to tell just such a cover story on the out-of-classroom place on our school landscape.

One difficult living and telling of this cover story occurred in midfall. During the years I taught at this school, we had often been chosen as a district site to be visited by local, national, and international visitors. That fall, a team of international researchers and teachers were scheduled for a 2-day visit to our school. For me, their visit began on a cold and snowy Sunday evening as I participated in a dinner party at my principal's home. As we ate, we dispersed in the kitchen, dining, family, and living rooms, clustering into small groups, telling stories of ourselves and the work we were engaged in. Our visitors were interested in learning more about our school and the larger city and district that surrounded it. Apart from introducing myself and telling our visitors the age level of children whom I worked with at the school, the conversation within my small cluster remained on the surface with little focus on the particularities of my current teaching assignment.

However, as we discussed the pros and cons of multi-age groupings and "at-risk" children, our conversation began to focus on meeting the increasingly diverse needs of children. As the last echoes of our thoughts about diversity and the needs of our children were fading, my principal joined our group and, picking up on what we were discussing, asked if I had shared how I was integrating curricula through metaphor and how this approach to planning was helping me to work effectively with the diverse range of children in my classroom. Knowing that this was not a safe place on the out-of-classroom landscape where I could speak of discontinuities and wonders such as those shaped by my story of Ameel and Monica, I responded to my principal's question by describing the surface of our in-classroom landscape; giving a brief description of how the colleague with whom I had planned the key idea and I had interwoven the various curricula into a variety of threads that allowed us to continue expanding the garden metaphor throughout the school year. I also gave a brief description of some of the activities we had been engaged in during the fall. There were sounds of interest and wonderings of whether I would share with them more about "the plan" during their 2-day visit. As our conversation came to a close, I knew that my telling of a cover story had gone unnoted. No one asked how this plan for the curriculum my children were expected to learn was working, or what sense the children seemed to be making of it, nor did I make any attempt to ask our visitors to listen to, or to help me think further about, the discontinuities I felt between these planned curriculum experiences and the stories I saw some of the children living out within our classroom context. Choosing to tell a cover story that left our visitors and my colleagues with the impression that life in our Year 1 and 2 classroom was indeed being successfully lived out as a caring classroom community, our conversation drew to a close.

This was the easy story to tell. Yet in telling it this way, I was only speaking "of the flat world where everything is safe, commonplace, and agreeable, the very small world about which we can all have consensus" (Metzger, 1992, p. 32).

Going Underground

Because Shaun and I lived inside this classroom and were immersed in the intimate details of the moments of each day, we knew that beneath what often appeared as a smooth surface, much tension, uncertainty, and discontinuity existed. For example, after working with the children for close to 2 months, we still saw things that concerned us: children being left out, hurting words being spoken by them to one another, and the persistent use of anger and aggression to "solve" problems with classmates or other children or adults in the school. Our concerns were significantly highlighted on the afternoon we helped Monica and Ameel think through their frustration and hurt with one another. I was stunned by the manner in which I saw Ameel live out his anger with his classmate. Our focus on thoughtful conversation seemed invisible alongside his loud, angry voice.

In the days ahead, scenes from this event replayed through my mind. In addition to recalling this scene, I began to recapture and replay angry images of the children from earlier in the fall. In the present, other incidents continued to occur. As I watched more and more of the children return inside with tears and angry stories, I began to dread the afternoon. Each afternoon we were spending larger amounts of time hearing the children tell angry stories about outside play times. For me, this created many discontinuities. According to our "teacher plan," this time was to be spent on a variety of shared reading activities—activities we rarely got to. What created the greatest sense of discontinuity for me, however, was that our in-classroom plans since the beginning of the school year had focused on creating a caring classroom community. As Shaun and I began to spend increasing time after school sharing our wonders about what we saw happening, we noticed that most of these incidents occurred when the children were outside, under other teachers' supervision and away from our in-classroom space. We wondered why these incidents occurred when we were not present. All fall we had talked with the children about caring for one another and had involved them in activities that, we thought, encouraged them to show how they cared for themselves and others. Each time the children came to us with hurt feelings or an unhappy story, we spent time talking with them. Shaun and I began to question what meaning these activities held for the children.

My sense of discomfort continued to center around two opposing thoughts. At times, I wished the children would learn to get along with one another and, in other moments, I wondered why these events were happening and what more could we do to encourage the children to care for one another. Days would pass during which I became ostrichlike, somewhere deep inside, hoping that incidents such as Ameel and Monica's would smooth themselves out, maybe even go away.

I felt trapped between the two voices conversing in my mind; one urged me to focus on the program of studies so as to ensure that the children were learning the material I was expected to teach, whereas the other continued to push me to look beneath the surface of what I was teaching and to uncover the stories the children were living.

After much talking and wondering what to do, Shaun and I decided to share our concerns with the children. The next day, we spent close to an hour talking with them. As always, their response to our concerns was thoughtful, as were the ways in which they responded to the concerns shared by some of the children in our classroom. At the end of the day, Shaun and I talked about what a moving experience it had been for us to listen to the children and to observe their interactions during our conversation. We both commented on the thoughtful nature of our dialogue and on how the conversation we had had that afternoon reminded us of the morning "support circle."

Listening to and Responding

As we thought further about that afternoon's conversation with the children, we decided to begin including a second support circle in the afternoon; one in which we would invite the children to share their concerns and celebrations about their school lives. We also decided to include a peace candle in order to create a sense of quiet thoughtfulness for the children as they returned to the in-classroom place after lunch playtime. The children already knew the peace candle as an important symbol within our classroom, for we used this candle to celebrate birthdays. When I initially brought the candle to school, the children quickly noticed that its holder looked like a globe of the world, and they eagerly promised to help take special care of it so that it would be part of our classroom for the entire year. They thought it interesting that the candle was placed into a sphere that had the raised shape of each continent on its outer edge. Some portions of the globe had been chiseled out, allowing light from the burning candle to shine.

When we discussed our idea of having a second support circle with the children, they eagerly agreed. We began the next afternoon sitting in a circle around the lit peace candle. The room was in darkness except for the rays of flickering light that shone through the open areas of the globe. The children were mesmerized; there was a feeling of peacefulness and caring as we talked about how this time in the support circle might be lived out. As our time in this space unfolded, the mutually negotiated construction of what might take place was an exciting process to be part of. Not only was the sense of support and caring that marked the morning support circle for "writing response" being carried over into the afternoon, other activities were also being introduced. Before long, Lucky (our class mascot) joined us and it became common practice for us to link hands with our neighbors when we settled into the circle formation. A new tradition was being shaped within our in-classroom place.

In the beginning, Shaun and I often prefaced the sharing by talking about something we wanted to celebrate or a concern we had about our in-classroom place. The children followed our lead, with examples of "I made a new friend today and it's Yazim" or "Valerie has my pencil and she won't give it back." Due to the unplanned and constructive nature of this space, our notions of what could occur continued to shift and expand and the range of what was considered acceptable continued to grow. Children soon began to offer response to classmates who shared school stories about not getting along or feeling left out. Their response was thoughtful and genuine. More than once, Shaun and I noticed how natural it seemed for the children to make sense of their concerns when they listened to classmates tell stories about them. One very moving experience of this occurred on the afternoon when one of our students, Tyler, was spending his last day with us.

Even though Tyler had attended kindergarten with many of the children who were in Year 1 in our classroom, he spent most of his school time being solitary. In the beginning it had been difficult to determine whether Tyler chose to live in this manner among his peers or whether they had chosen this position for him. Early in the year, we noticed the ways in which other children looked across the room at one another when we were rearranging groups and Tyler was placed into *their* group. We began to expect that, within a few minutes, the children in Tyler's new group would come to us and say that he was humming, shaking his pencil, or drumming his desktop and they could not concentrate. We would encourage these children to involve Tyler in the activities and, although some tried hard to do this, he remained isolated. When we talked with Tyler about how he imagined his time in our classroom, he would look at us with a smile, responding with various versions of "I don't know." Some days, Tyler would arrive in the classroom after the morning recess and then spend the remainder of the day running around the room, hiding under his desk, or hugging his knees to his chest and rocking back and forth while softly singing in his first language.

On the morning of the day when Tyler suddenly left our classroom, his mother brought him to school and asked us to send all of his belongings home with him. She told us that they were moving to another province the next day. Not only were Shaun and I stunned by Tyler's family's sudden departure but we ached inside, knowing we would no longer have contact with Tyler. All morning he sat beneath his desk, refusing to come out or to join in the day's activities. Finally, he crawled out from underneath his desk and walked over to the coat area on one side of the classroom. From behind the partial wall that enclosed this space, Tyler's voice, rising and fading, called, "Mmmmrrrrrsssss. Huuuuuuuuuuuuber; Mmmmrrrrrsssss. Huuuuuuuuuuuuber." Each time I walked behind the wall, knelt down beside him where he was curled up underneath the coat hooks, and asked him what he wanted, his only response was a smile.

That afternoon we began our support circle by telling the children that Tyler was moving the next day and that this was his last afternoon in our classroom. By the looks on the children's faces, we knew they were as shocked as we had been. Shaun and I suggested that we might spend some of our time saying good-bye to Tyler and wishing him well. Immediately there was a rush of bodies, and Tyler was surrounded by his classmates, all talking at once, telling him how they liked having him in our classroom and how much they would miss him. I remember the sense of both relief and surprise I felt as I observed the children. I had no idea that so many of his classmates would respond to him as they did. Before long, several of the children were crying, as was Tyler. He sat for a moment and then looked slowly around. In a quiet voice he said, "I don't want to leave but my mom says we have to."

Crossing Boundaries

Our afternoon support circles had begun with a focus on the out-of-classroom place, namely the playground, and how this frustration was shaping events in our in-classroom space, but our storytelling and figuring out soon began to cross the boundary, marked by our children and our in-classroom place, to include stories of children from other classrooms, events occurring across the landscape of our school, as well as stories shaped through their out-of-school experiences.

One such crossing occurred on an afternoon in which one of the children "storied" pushing one another in the lines they formed as they waited to come back inside after recess. As we continued to unravel the events of this story, we heard rumblings of "Why do we have to line up" coming from some of the children. I remember my feelings as I looked around the circle at the children, wondering, "Should we explore this further or change the subject?" After deciding to continue, I asked the children what they would suggest if someone asked them how they thought we might move from the out-of-school space into the in-school space. They responded by telling me that when they went to the nearby mall with their parents, they were not required to line up before being invited to enter, but, instead, merely opened the doors and walked in. We ended our conversation that afternoon by deciding, as a class, that rather than having one long line, we would make two shorter ones. They understood that the first two children who arrived at the entrance would have the remainder of their classmates lining up behind them.

As we sat in the support circle another afternoon, our conversation began to focus on Hat Day, a school-wide contest that had occurred earlier in the week. The outcome of this event had been that the classroom with the highest percentage of children wearing hats to school on that day was honored at an assembly and their picture was taken for a bulletin board posting highlights of the event and this one classroom's victory. Kyle's hand was stretching higher and higher as our conversation on Hat Day continued. When I invited Kyle to share, he said that he wished that our classroom had won Hat Day. I asked him why he felt that way. Kyle explained that he wanted our class to have our picture in the hallway just like the classroom that had won. Jamie responded to Kyle by saying that he felt bad because our classroom had lost. Sam responded to both boys by saying that he thought Hat Day should not have been a contest but just a fun day. Amidst a chorus of "Yeah, I agree with Sam," I asked Sam to share more of his thoughts. He explained that he thought it was unfair that one class won the contest, because it made students in the other classrooms in the school feel bad when they lost, and, he continued, "They might think they aren't as important." I was intrigued by Sam's sense of "importantness" and asked him to say more. He continued by saying that "even on his birthday," his parents gave his little sister a present because she did not yet understand what birthdays were and they did not want her to feel left out, which she would if only Sam received presents.

Then, one afternoon, a story was shared in our support circle that took us deeper into the underground than we had ever traveled before. This story grabbed us, causing the boundaries that had once constrained our storytelling to become less visible. We were immediately taken to a landscape that although not unrecognizable, was somewhat unfamiliar territory. The telling of this story dramatically changed the surface of our classroom landscape for the remainder of the school year. Ameel had just returned to school after being away due to the death of his grandfather. We began that afternoon by my welcoming Ameel back to our support circle and saying that we hoped that the caring of his school family would help to ease the hurt he was feeling inside. Ameel immediately put his hand up indicating that he wanted to share. His voice quivered as he spoke. He told his classmates how he had been away because his grandfather had died. He explained that he had spent the past week at his grandparents' home saying good-bye to his grandfather. He described the rituals his culture performed when someone dies. With tears flowing down his cheeks he ended his story by saying that he was worried about his dad; he had never seen him cry before. As Ameel's voice dropped off, many hands came up. We spent the reminder of our time hearing and responding to the children tell their own personal stories of death.

The telling of Ameel's story changed the landscape of our classroom in a general way but it had a most noticeable impact on the storying that occurred in our afternoon support circles for the remainder of the school year. No longer did Shaun or I have to preface these with a topic. Ameel had taken the risk to share a very personal story that he wanted his classmates to respond to and to help him think further about, and his classmates slowly began to follow his lead. Our stories shifted from school stories, from surface stories such as "Last night I went to McDonalds and look what I got," and from stories about how the out-of-classroom places on the school landscape were shaping our in-classroom place, to stories about the very personal, real issues and concerns we were all living through. Concerns such as death, divorce, unemployment, and family difficulties to wonderings or theories about how and why events in the physical and manufactured world occur as they do became important threads in our conversations. With each shift regarding how our time in the support circle could be lived out, our conversation moved deeper into the underground; uncovering important self-truths that were shaping the surface of our classroom landscape. Listening to the stories we told shifted our understanding of the possibilities for living community on the in-classroom place of our classroom landscape.

CHAPTER 3

Traveler on a Journey

Karen Whelan

*A journey awaits you. It is one filled with possibility and meaning. It
will call you to come to know who you are and where you are going.
At times you will need to share this pathway, whereas at others, you
will travel alone. You will make many important choices at crossroads along the way. Each step will carry you toward new discoveries, so step with great care.*

The Journey: A Metaphor to Guide Me

The metaphor of the journey has become significant to me as I have
reflected on my past 7 years as a teacher. It provides me a pathway on which
to travel as I try to frame my experiences. I will borrow this metaphor as I
share stories of my experiences with the conferencing process at both the
elementary and junior high level. These stories move on and off different
pathways, from the in-classroom place to the out-of-classroom place on the
landscape. At times, the pathways seem to merge together, moving harmo-
niously in the same direction. At other times, they seem to travel parallel paths,
moving forward but separately. At still other moments, these pathways di-
verge and move abruptly away from one another. As a teacher who has experienced these multiple pathways, recognizing and naming these differences,
I am enabled to see the significant influence the out-of-classroom place has
had on my in-classroom practice and on my evolving teacher identity.

One of my most recent stops along my journey was at our annual
Teachers' Convention, where fellow travelers gather each year to listen, to
learn, and to share their stories. As I wander around the convention center,
I can see teachers in small, circular clusters and intimate pairs. In this place

away from their school landscapes, teachers come together in a network of safety and support, finding the luxury of time and space to enter into meaningful conversations with one another. As they break away from these interactions and move into the larger presentations, they are challenged by the messages being delivered by prominent educational leaders. At one of these sessions I listened intently as a highly respected educator within my school district cast "student-led conferences" in a negative light. I left this session feeling discouraged and frustrated; I felt as though the experiences upon which I based my practice were being devalued. I have learned that the influence of these key stakeholders on the out-of-classroom place on the landscape permeates our schools and classrooms and the lives of teachers and children. This is a reality I am still trying to make sense of in my journey as a teacher.

Stepping Out: My Beginnings as a Teacher

There will be moments when you find yourself in darkened valleys where your fears and uncertainties seem to overcome you. Have faith . . . you will find a passage out and you will climb to new vantage points, see new horizons that will nurture renewed strength within you.

It was a cold December just a few short days before Christmas when I received the call that marked the beginning of a new journey in my life. I heard: "Karen, congratulations. We appreciated our interview with you and would like to offer you the Grade One position at our school beginning in January." It was the realization of a dream for me, one that I had held close to my heart for as far back as I could remember. I was actually going to be a real teacher, in my own classroom filled with real children!

I spent that entire Christmas holiday shaping my new classroom, which had previously been used as a storage space for the school. I cleaned out the room from floor to ceiling. I dragged in old bookshelves from dusty corners of the school and started to create what I had always dreamed a classroom could be. I set up centers and moved desks around several times until they felt just right. I put carpet down on the tile floor to create a warm, cozy place for the children and me to gather, to sing songs, tell stories, and read books. Daily, I arrived at the school with something new to brighten the learning environment for the children I would be teaching. Each little treasure seemed to bring me closer to a world that I had once only imagined.

Finally, the day I had so long been waiting for arrived. I arrived at the school at 6:30 in the morning on my first day. I had to figure out how to turn off the alarm as I entered the building even before the school custodian. I wrote my entire lessons for the morning on the chalkboard in a little corner just in case I might forget what I was supposed to be doing.

With all my preparation for my first day completed, I sat down at my desk. The school was still and quiet on that early January morning. I looked out over my classroom, focusing on the empty desks, which sat side by side in a U formation, knowing that in a few short hours those desks would be filled with young children waiting for me, their teacher, to begin their day. I remember this moment well, for it was the first time I was filled with the profound understanding that I really was a teacher.

The days passed quickly for the children and me. We spent our mornings together reading and writing and sharing our stories. At center time the children moved off to different locations throughout the classroom to work with one another and to shape some of their own learning experiences. Some went to listening stations to hear stories, others to math centers to explore a concept. A larger group would gather at the reading/writing centers where a variety of colored paper, crayons, stamps, and other materials were set up to allow the children to capture and celebrate their stories.

With a small class size of 15 children, I was free to work with every child on a personal basis each day. I began to collect rich samples of their work in math and language arts (the two subjects I was responsible for teaching). I even found time to tape-record each child's progress with reading over the months I spent with them. These too were added to my collection of materials that celebrated each child's personal journey. We were tucked away in our special classroom with our door shut to the outside world. Together, we were building a magical place and we were happy.

March arrived quickly and, with it, parent-teacher interviews (as they were then defined). I felt eager and somewhat nervous at the same time: eager to share all the rich information gathered about each child, and nervous because I was plunging blindly into an experience I had never been a part of—not even as a child in my twelve years of schooling.

I recall seeking out my colleagues to find out how it all worked. "Ten minutes," they said, "and keep to a strict timeline. Otherwise you'll leave parents waiting in the hallway."

"You may even want to set an egg timer so that they know when their time is up," another responded.

"Just discuss the marks and tell generally how the child is doing. That's all they really want to know."

It was with this guidance that I, as a beginning teacher, confronted my first "interview" experience with parents. My files of student work sat untouched. There certainly was no time to share the richness of what lay within them. Instead we looked at check marks and As, Bs and Cs on the report card. In an attempt to capture the beauty of who each child was through my eyes, I had included handwritten anecdotal comments with each child's report card. The marks, however, seemed to negate these pages. The parents wanted to know mainly about the marks and where their child's "B" stood in comparison to the rest of the class.

The questions I received were not what I had been anticipating. I really thought they would want to know more about their child's experiences in our classroom; whether the child loved to read or write stories, who his or her special friends were, to see and cherish the work their child was creating. I felt relieved after the interviews were over. It was a tiring and unfulfilling process, and I wondered what the parents had really taken away with them. What profile of their child had I really provided? What sense did they have of what took place within our classroom community? Did they have faith in who I was as a teacher in their child's life? If only I had found the time to celebrate their child with them, how differently they would have experienced the growth of their child in his or her first year of school. How sad that they missed out on the rich, cherished moments that were a part of every day that the children and I spent together.

In this, my first teaching experience, I followed blindly on a path that had no internal sense of direction for me. It was only later in my career that I would come to realize what a profound impact these beginning experiences would have in shaping my beliefs and practice about the sharing and celebration of student learning and growth.

Companions on the Journey

As you travel to new places, you will learn much from those who have walked these trails before you. They will provide you with direction, yet they will respect your journey and let you find your own way. They are the travelers of days gone by and they have much wisdom to share with you. Listen to their voices and learn alongside them.

From the moment I arrived at my second school, I knew that it was a place that believed in building relationships and creating a connected feeling between children, parents, and teachers. The way in which student-learning conferences were structured reflected this belief. They were designed to create a space in which all could have a voice. Children were the focal point and the key communicators as they celebrated their learning and growth with their parents and teachers. The teacher and parents served as facilitators or coaches, providing support and encouragement to the child as he or she shared his or her thoughts. It was expected that the conferences be a minimum of a half hour in length to provide time for the celebration of learning. The style or flow of the conference was never structured or mandated to "look" a certain way.

In fact, we were encouraged to sit in on other conferences just so we could see how uniquely we were all approaching them as a staff. Even within our classrooms, we recognized that every child experienced the conference differently. The diversity that existed within the learning process was also transferred to the sharing process, which was a vital part of the conference. I was taken under the wings of two very special teachers, who helped me shape my conferences into meaningful experiences for all. They listened to my concerns and understood my fears as coming from a teacher new to this process. Their open sharing guided me forward on my journey, and helped me find a process that felt just right.

My Story of Sarah

I am not quite certain how to capture the story of Sarah in words, but I know that it is an important story to tell because it uncovers part of the richness found in the conferencing process that was introduced to me at my second school while I was still very much a "beginner" in my teaching journey.

Our last conference together marked the end of a 2-year journey for Sarah, myself, and her parents. She had been a part of our Year 3–4 learning community, in which I remained her teacher over a 2-year period.

Sarah was a beautiful girl with long brown hair, bright eyes, and a smile that brought out my affections. She had a gentle personality and was always reaching out to children in need. Sarah loved to write poetry, as did her father. She carried a small notebook with her everywhere she went. It was not uncommon to find her snuggled up next to a tree at recess time jotting down notes about the world around her. Later, she would compose these thoughts and feelings into beautiful poetry that captured her experiences. Sarah was one of those special students who, for whatever reason, touched me in a very deep way. I was able to see my reflection in Sarah's eyes, in her actions, in the way she made sense of the experiences being shaped in our classroom.

There was something magical about those beginning years as a teacher that I have since lost. I am not sure if it was the "newness" of everything or maybe just my own naïveté and idealism, but everything seemed so fresh and exciting. Sarah was a part of those first beginning experiences in my classroom. She traveled with me as I tried to make sense of who I was becoming as a teacher. Perhaps this is why it was so very difficult for all of us to say good-bye at our final conference that June.

We gathered at a round table near the back of the classroom. Sarah sat opposite me, and her mother and father sat on either side of her. There was warmth, familiarity, and safety in this circular formation, much as in a family gathering at the supper table. As I watched Sarah celebrating her growth, I could not help but think about how this sharing signified the end of our journey together. This was the culmination of 2 years of shared memories. It was an important conference—a sacred one.

After Sarah had finished sharing, I tried to respond to her as I had always done in the past at previous conferences, but my words would not come and were replaced with tears. Sarah got up from the table and walked over to sit in my lap. We all cried then; Sarah, her parents and I . . . we knew it was time to say good-bye.

It was about a week later that Sarah came to me with this poem that she and her father composed together. It helped both of us understand why we had to say good-bye, and it allowed me to take a beautiful part of Sarah with me.

A time to say good-bye
Two years is not a long time
But long enough for our hearts to shine
You showed me and taught me the right ways
I'm glad that you were mine
Over the two years we had good times and some bad times
too
Now with tissue over my eyes to try to dry my tears
I wish you well—for words cannot say what hearts can do
well
Now as I turn the pages of the book of my life
I shall keep a book mark on these pages
So many memories I shall share
I hold them so close to my heart
Now I wish we could never go apart
But like a baby bird I have to learn
to leave the nest behind to see if I can fly
So all I can say for now
Is thank you and good bye.

Love,
Sarah Plummer (1991)

My six conferences with Sarah and her parents over a 2-year period were connecting experiences that allowed us to grow closer. These sacred moments enabled us to come to know one another on a personal level, and each conference sent an important message to Sarah:

You are precious . . .
    Worth taking time for . . .
A celebration to behold.
    We gather to listen to your voice.
We come so that we may know you,
    treasure you.
You are someone special.

The learning conferences at this school were rich growth experiences for everyone involved. They provided the children with the opportunity to articulate and demonstrate what they had learned within the context of their work in a particular classroom community. The parents were able to make sense of their child's growth through participating in the sharing and discussion that flowed within this mutually constructed safe and caring space. The teacher was able to celebrate and marvel at the way in which the child was able to express his or her understanding of his or her learning experiences.

The pathways on the in-classroom and out-of-classroom place on the landscape seemed to merge at this school. The experiences shaped at conferences became important stories shared in the staff room and hallways. Teachers found strength in one another as they listened and responded to these stories. We knew what we believed in and we knew that the parents and children valued it as well. Together, we created shared common ground, expansive enough for the differences of many to be held and nurtured.

Shaping New Paths: From Elementary into Junior High

You will build lasting relationships as you share the path with others, and you will discover the strength that comes when you walk hand in hand with friends. At times you may need to follow, and at others you will be called to lead, and the bridges you build together will be strong and will take you to new common ground.

If you have not yet experienced the "corral method" of conferencing that predominates within junior high and high school settings, let me paint a picture for you, the parent: You enter a large gymnasium area, and before you stands a mass of humanity. Your first thought is that you must be in the wrong place; perhaps you have the date wrong and this is really the flea market event. Much to your surprise, as you look around more carefully, you realize that indeed you are in the right place. On the walls, behind rows of tables, are names of teachers, listed in alphabetical order. You shuffle yourself quickly into a line of other parents, hoping to speak with a least one of your child's teachers. You wait, and wait some more. Finally you arrive at your "stall." There are parents on either side of you and several standing directly behind you. You are surrounded! You speak fast and in whispered tones. "Why has my child's mark dropped so dramatically?" you ask. After the teacher has figured out exactly *who* your child is, a collection of marks is shown to you and some attempt is made at an explanation. Five minutes later, with the sound of impatient toe tapping from other parents in line behind you, you are strongly encouraged to "move along." You do so, left with only a vague sense of what your child is experiencing in school.

I empathize with junior high and high school teachers who live through this method of conferencing. They are often forced into this structure because of the vast number of students they teach on a weekly basis. Theirs is a cattle path; one they follow because of the tradition of schooling at this level. This brings me to my story of conferencing during my junior high teaching experience. Here we brought our elementary and junior high experiences together to get off the cattle path, and to envision something different.

Taking on new and exciting challenges in my life seems to be a pattern that started early in my career and stayed with me. My plunge into junior high, however, was an endeavor that took me a little by surprise. I was filled with a fair bit of anxiety the summer before I began. I started having nightmares about tough kids dressed in black leather jackets, smoking cigarettes in front of the school. I can remember watching kids intently whenever I was out in the shopping malls, hoping to catch some glimpse of what adolescents looked like. I had not been around teenagers since I had been one myself. My fear and apprehension stayed with me right up until my first day of school. When I finally met my class, I realized that they were just young people and not the monsters of my nightmares after all.

It was an exciting time within this junior high setting. We were a brand new school, building our vision from the ground up. We decided to shape the Year 7 program as a core program. This meant that the students would spend the majority of the school day with one teacher who would program for them in all of the core subject areas. This would enable us to come to know our students on a more personal level and to provide programming for them in a more connected way. Our team of Year 7 teachers included people with diverse backgrounds and expertise in all the core areas. This team support allowed us to lean on one another. Although our teaching team was not without its trials and tribulations, connected and meaningful relationships evolved for all five of us that year.

When the inevitable topic of communicating student growth came up at our staff meeting, there was a great deal of discussion on what it might look like. The Year 8 and 9 teachers wanted to work with 15-minute interviews. This is what they knew and understood, and they were working with larger numbers of students. The Year 7 teachers decided to follow the elementary style of conference reporting in which the child acted as the key communicator in the celebration of learning and the parents and teacher became active participants and supporters alongside them.

My Story of Tina

One of the most memorable experiences I had with conferencing at the junior high level was with my most challenging student, Tina. Tina came to me with many learning difficulties and many insecurities about how she would cope with the junior high curriculum. These insecurities caused her to act out with aggression and to approach her learning experiences with disinterest. I can recall feeling quite alarmed when I learned that Tina had entered into a fistfight with an older student at the lockers on the very first day of school. For all of these reasons, I knew that our first conference together would be a critical one.

I met with Tina and her parents early in the school year to discuss the special programming that would be necessary in order to meet her needs and to encourage success in her learning. We gathered together at a table in our classroom and began to get to know one another. Through our conversation, we discovered a connection between our two families. One of my close relatives, a special education teacher, had taught Tina's older sibling, Kelly, who was cognitively disabled. Learning about Tina's family background was important to my understanding of her own feelings of inadequacy. This kind of personal dialogue could only take place in the security of our classroom, where we had time and privacy.

As the conversation continued, I began to notice that Tina was becoming somewhat uncomfortable. She stared down at the table and nervously twisted the rings on her fingers. When I asked if she was OK, she responded by saying, "I was supposed to go to this other school where retarded people go, you know. That's where Kelly is now." Tina knew that she was different from her older sibling, and she wanted desperately to feel that she belonged with her peers in our Year 7 classroom.

Her parents took time to express their hopes and dreams for Tina. They wanted her to succeed and feel happy, to have a normal adolescent experience. Tina's mother spoke of her love for her daughter and her desire for Tina to have choices in her life when she finished school. "Tina has strengths she can use," she said passionately. "I want her to build these strengths in school."

At this point I went over to my desk and picked up the large green binder sent over from Tina's elementary school. Her eyes lit up when I showed it to her, and her parents had knowing smiles on their faces. She gently opened it as though it were a rare treasure. She began showing me drawings, writing, and other pieces of her previous learning experiences, which dated back to her beginnings in kindergarten. I watched Tina's face as she proudly shared a part of who she was. These were the strengths her mother had spoken of, the ones I knew I could build on if I worked in cooperation with Tina and her parents over the year ahead.

The green binder was indeed a treasure, for it held memories for Tina and her parents of her elementary life, allowing her to story these experiences in meaningful ways. I learned that day that this young adolescent was much more than that tough girl who had thrown a punch on her first day of school. She was Tina, a girl who had struggled through school and who desperately wanted to fit in and feel "accepted."

Within this junior high context, Tina's story had a space to be told. As teachers of these young people, we were all allowed voice in shaping what worked best for ourselves and our students. We respected one another's decisions to go with a style of conferencing that made sense for us, recognizing that at each grade level the circumstances differed because of the number of students we each taught. Our pathways ran parallel to one another's, different enough to honor the grade level at which we worked, yet still moving toward common ground in what we believed and valued about student learning and growth.

I am thankful to this day that we never resorted to the corral method. Instead, we mutually constructed a landscape that enabled children, parents, and teachers to give voice to the teaching and learning process. Like my previous school, this new setting became a place where diversity in style was celebrated.

Two years after my junior high experience, on a warm June afternoon, I received a phone call at my new school. "Miss Whelan, is that you?" a familiar, loud voice piped over the line. "It's Tina! Do you remember me? I was thinking maybe you could come to my graduation?"

The Road Less Traveled: Listening to My Inner Voice

You will find your journey's end where you will celebrate discoveries with others in the world around you. You will have rich stories to tell of the experiences you have lived, and you will know, within your heart, that this ending point marks the place of yet another beginning.

My final story on this narrative journey brings me to my present school landscape, in which I face two diverging roads much like those described by Robert Frost (in Untermeyer, 1956) in his poem "The Road Not Taken." My beginning experiences with the conferencing process were tentative and uncertain, and my end point is no more clear. I find myself at a crossroads in my journey with the conferencing process: If I move in one direction, I follow the norm and "buckle under" to the ever increasing pressures with which I am faced outside the classroom. If I choose the other path, I will at least honor what I have come to know, but I will most surely travel alone.

When I reflect on the discomfort and unrest I have felt over the past few years in this profession, I can attribute a great deal of it to the climate that exists in the out-of-classroom place on the landscape. With a greater emphasis on test results, marks, and improving student achievement in an efficient manner, I find myself being tugged and pulled in so many different directions. As a traveler on this journey, my backpack has become heavy; filled with the practices, wishes, and demands of others. Perhaps I can lighten the load by sharing one final story.

As in my previous junior high school, this staff was brought together to shape a school from the ground up. We were an energetic group with strong opinions about what we felt was important in the lives of young children. Around early October of our first year, we began discussing report cards and the conferencing process. There was great debate about whether we should go with the half-hour student-led conferences or the open-house style of conferencing. This is where the path diverged for many of us. Several teachers wanted to go with the open-house conference in which up to six families at a time can be present in the room. This type of conference surfaced in our district mainly as a way to save teachers time from the many hours required in the half-hour conferencing process. I invite you down this path to see one possible vantage point of the open-house conferencing process.

It is an evening in November; a single night set aside for celebrating learning at the school. The building has been cleaned from floor to ceiling and children's desks tidied in preparation for the event. I peer into a classroom and I see children and their parents seated tightly together, trying to create meaningful spaces for authentic sharing. Parents and teachers talk in hushed tones about learning difficulties and special needs, perhaps fearful that others may overhear. One parent is distracted from her own child's sharing as she listens to the articulate presentation being made by another child nearby. Is she silently wondering why her child does not display this same confidence? Children take their parents around the room to try to show them special centers and personal work. They are faced with lines and crowded spaces. One shy child stands hesitantly outside the classroom door. I wonder if sharing in large groups is difficult for her. I watch as she slowly enters the classroom, unsure of herself in this sea of unfamiliar faces.

The progress-report document lies across the desks of the children in the classroom. It has been written in isolation, separate from the child and the parents, and the comments on it seem foreign to them as they read through it. I watch as families become absorbed with this written document, using much of their half hour of blocked time trying to make sense of what it is saying about who their child is. I wonder if parents leave these conferences frustrated, not knowing whether the teacher truly knows their child's personal gifts and individual needs.

In our first year of operation at this school, we were free to go with a style of conferencing that best suited us and our children. From there we moved to a "locked-in" format in which we would run personal conferences in November and open-house conferences in March. My greatest concern was that, as a group of professionals with a variety of different personal strengths and talents, we talked ourselves into believing that there was one right way to hold a conference at structured times throughout the school year. In our first year, when some teachers stayed with the individual conferences whereas others went with the open-house style, the climate at conferencing time became somewhat tense. There was little acceptance of our diverging paths, and difference became a threat on our school landscape. This kind of strain is too much, particularly in difficult times, and so I found myself following the trail chosen by the majority rather than choosing for myself. When you become weary as a traveler, sometimes it is easier to follow along in silence than it is to listen to your own voice. I cannot help but think about what important parts of myself I leave behind on the trail when this occurs.

This struggle led me to a great deal of reflection. I found myself looking inward and questioning why I had such strong feelings about the conferencing process. I came to recognize that my resistance had been ignited by others telling me how to approach something in which I had already invested a great deal of time as a teacher. It was through honoring each child's unique personality and development that I have been able to find meaning and value in the conferencing process. I knew each child on a personal level and I trusted my own judgment. More and more as I am told what to do and how to do it in my profession, I find myself losing sight of who I am and what I know.

When I reflect back to my beginning story of the Teachers' Convention, I recognize that it was this experience that awakened me from my blind travels on a trail that was no longer my own. Hearing those from the outside placing little value in my voice, and in what I have come to know as a teacher, enabled me to journey back over my teaching experience and discover the messages embedded within my stories as a teacher on shifting school landscapes.

I take these experiences and stories with me as I continue my travels as a teacher. No one can take them from me or tell me that they are not valuable. I have lived these stories and I know their worth.

CHAPTER 4

Nancy's Conflicting Story
of Teaching in Her Professional
Knowledge Landscape

Sally Quan, JoAnn Phillion,
and Ming Fang He

In this chapter, Sally, JoAnn, and Ming Fang share a story of Nancy, a nurse educator from Lakeview College, a community college in a metropolitan area of Canada. This story reveals the complexity of Nancy's life in her professional knowledge landscape. As we heard more stories from this landscape we began to understand that Nancy's everyday teaching life shifted with social and economic changes in society, changes in her institution, and changes in her life and in the lives of her students.

Sally negotiated her entry into Nancy's class in 1994. Sally, a registered nurse trained in the Philippines, received graduate education in Canada and taught nursing education for 20 years. Lakeview College, where she taught and did her research with Nancy, offers postdiploma-program certificate courses such as critical care nursing, operating room nursing for registered nurses who wish to pursue further education, and a refresher/upgrading nursing course for graduates from other countries who wish to qualify for registration to practice in Canada. The refresher portion of the program is designed to enhance the knowledge and skills of registered nurses who have been away from nursing practice for more than 5 years. Students enrolled in the upgrading program are graduate nurses who obtained their education outside of the province. One purpose of the upgrading portion of the program is to augment the knowledge and skills of foreign-accredited nurses. This course is a prerequisite to taking the registered nurse (RN) examination. The program has four components: medical-surgical, pediatrics, psychiatry, and maternal-newborn.

Nancy, a nurse educator with whom Sally did research for one and a half years, had been teaching the core component, Medical-Surgical Nursing, for 9 years. Sally did her research with Nancy and two accredited nurses from the Philippines in Nancy's class. Sally visited her participants an average of once a week, attended classes, and observed in the Learning Resource Center and the clinical area. She taped interviews, wrote fieldnotes, had informal conversations with students and Nancy, and attended meetings. She found Nancy and the students very welcoming and accommodating. Students joked with Nancy and one another, which was something that many immigrant students might not be used to doing in their native countries. For example, in the Philippines, there is a certain distance maintained between the teacher and the student. The teacher is thought of as the source of all knowledge. It is almost impossible for students to question teachers.

With over forty students in her class, Nancy had decided that the lecture method was the most expedient way to get through the volume of information that her students needed in order to be able to pass the RN exam. However, since the majority of the students in the class spoke English as a second language and came from dramatically different nursing education and cultural backgrounds, it was hard for them to understand the language, concepts, and terminology that Nancy was using. These students spoke Tagalog, Arabic, Cantonese, Polish, Ukrainian, Russian, English, French, Spanish, and other languages. These students felt pressured to pass the RN exam to become qualified to practice in Canada. They were required to attend many hours of class and clinical practice each week, and learn a large amount of material in a short period of time. At the same time, they had to work long hours in order to support their families.

As Sally developed a strong relationship with Nancy and these students, JoAnn and Ming Fang were invited to join the research in Nancy's class. One day when we walked into the classroom, we saw over 40 students lined up in rows in the narrow, cramped room. Students jostled each other to get front-row seats. Child-size desks filled all the available floor space. Hospital beds with green plastic covers were pushed against one wall. Nancy stood at the front of the room between the first row of students and the blackboard. She turned to us and said, "Look! They're on top of me, there's only three feet between the front of the class and the blackboard. I find myself not looking at the students in the front row because they're too close to me." Nancy was frustrated with this situation. Since 1994 she had been fighting for a larger room but had been unable to obtain one, although the number of foreign-accredited nurses in her refresher/upgrading program continued to increase.

The students checked with each other about assignments in their native languages. Nancy smiled and suggested, "Speak English, please!" To us, she said: "I tell the students to speak English when in the classroom so they can practice speaking the English language. But the students continue to speak their native language. I find it disrespectful to others who do not speak their language. This is complicated by the fact that there are so many languages spoken at the same time. This is disruptive." The students looked at her and went on talking.

Nancy circulated in the front rows calling students by name. She turned to one student and asked, "How is your dad doing? Will you be going to Mexico to visit him?" As Nancy collected personal history questionnaires from the previous class, she said, "Now I am going to be able to find out all about your lives." She laughed. Some students smiled. She walked around the room and chatted with students about what they had done in the previous class. She told us that the students had been put in groups and had discussed multicultural issues in nursing. The discussion had gone so well that when Nancy went back and asked the students if they wanted to continue, they chose to work in groups for the whole class. They told Nancy that they had enjoyed the discussion because they could share personal experiences. She asked the students if they felt they had learned a lot when they were in the groups. Ana, an accredited nurse from the Philippines, nodded her head and murmured to her partner in Tagalog that she had learned a lot. Nancy said to the class, "I wish we had more time to have small-group discussions. Unfortunately we only have 12 weeks; the lecture format works best." As Nancy talked with the students, she took attendance. She usually did so in this informal manner rather than following institutional rules, in the belief that this method was more appropriate for her adult students.

Before she started the class, Nancy gave some instructions about what the students needed to study in preparation for the exam. She said, "It is a midterm exam and it will take place next week. I think it is on Monday, I am not exactly sure." She kiddingly said, "Don't tell Greta (the dean) about this. This exam will be set up like the nursing registration examination. The topics will include growth and development." She also warned the students to expect questions on intravenous calculations and medications. There would be a case study of a patient with respiratory problems. This patient was gay and HIV positive. She alerted them to the fact that this patient would need counseling in addition to nursing care. This case would go beyond physical care into emotional care. She also mentioned that there would be questions about a case of rheumatoid arthritis. "You also need to know about lupus," Nancy added. Some students whispered to each other, "What's that?" She turned to the class and insisted, "Oh, yes, you know it because we've covered it in class." Some students looked confused, and they checked with their neighbors in their native languages. She referred to Graves disease and fractures and noted that the students needed to understand the care of patients with fracture. "You need to review the muscular system," she said. "In addition to the fracture, the patient developed tuberculosis; so you can see how they build a case incorporating different factors." She told the students that cataracts and glaucoma would be covered. Some students exclaimed, "Oh, no!" Nancy apologized, "Oh, we have not covered this in class." She then told the students to cross it out. The students were concerned about the upcoming test on Monday, it being a midterm exam. They were being given a bonus quiz that day. Nancy explained the grading system. The students seemed to have difficulty understanding exactly how the bonus quiz system points worked. Some students were worried about the multiple choice format, which they had never faced in their native countries.

Nancy told her students that the class for the morning was on principles of teaching and learning. She hurried through a series of overheads that contained dense information with such terminology as *randomized*, *intertwined*, *transition*, *optimum*, *acquisition*, *relevance*, *facilitator*, *modality*, and *acuity*. The students murmured as the overheads flashed by. She introduced the topic by saying that nurses in Canada were expected to teach their patients about diet, exercise, medication, taking blood pressure, and changing wound dressings. She explained that teaching principles and learning principles were intertwined. She asked, "How many students are having difficulty when they sit in this class and why?" Some students complained that it was the first time they had to sit for such a long time in a class. Some remarked that usually when they studied in their countries they sat in rows and did independent work. Most students took notes word for word and tried to keep pace with Nancy.

Nancy continued to skim through overheads. She talked about different learners having different skills and different learning strategies. "As a teacher and nurse, you always have to consider your client and their different learning styles." She emphasized that a nurse was a teacher and a learner. After she put up a list of three types of learning—psychomotor, affective, and cognitive—Nancy moved on to internal and external factors that affected learning. She displayed a list of learning principles:

1. Relevance of learning
2. Progression from simple to complex
3. Appropriate level of anxiety
4. Active involvement in the learning process
5. Success in learning
6. Feedback on performance

Then she asked, "What is learning?" Some students were silent; others began to whisper to one another in their various languages. Nancy read from another overhead, "Learning is the acquiring of knowledge or skills." The students were busy with copying the overheads.

The class was dismissed for a 20-minute coffee break. During this, Nancy told us that in the previous semester, six students had repeated her course and failed again. Some other students passed her course but failed the RN Exam. In the hallway, we joined a group of students who were talking. Sally introduced us to Ana, one of the participants in her thesis research. When we asked Ana how she was doing in the course, she told us: "I failed the RN Exam before. I am very worried about failing again." She continued:

> The RN exams are really for Canadians, but Canada has a multi-cultural population with different religious backgrounds, different family orientations, different traditions and practices. And even diet and nutrition, how would I know that there's rhubarb? There's no rhubarb back home. Back home we don't openly talk about sex. I mean, it doesn't come up for discussion. There was a question on the exam about which is the safest position for a person who has a spinal injury. Those are the sort of questions that are not really in the book. I mean, you can't find the answer in the book. They [teachers] say it's basic nursing knowledge but I don't know if it is. It's not in the book. It's very frustrating actually because it [the RN exam] is completely different from the exam in the Phil [Philippines]. There are many barriers: cultural and language barriers as well as exam styles. You know in Philippines we never did multiple choice exams! I could speak English . . . I could write English but it's not enough. I did my best but as far as nursing is concerned, it's different because of these barriers. I get trapped in these troubled areas.

Ana obtained her bachelor of science in nursing from one of the most prestigious universities in the Philippines. Nursing graduates at this university often rank in the top ten in the national nursing board examination. Ana worked as a hospital nurse and a company nurse, and as a representative for a pharmaceutical company in Manila. Four years ago she had come to Canada as a nanny, leaving behind her husband and their 2-year-old daughter. This is not uncommon, as many Filipinos trained in a variety of professions, such as teaching, nursing, medicine, engineering, and business, go abroad as domestic workers to support their families at home. One year ago, Ana became a landed immigrant. She immediately started the process of sponsoring her husband and daughter to join her in Canada. In the meantime, she continued to send money to her family. She quit her full-time job as a nanny and took a part-time job at a fast-food restaurant in order to prepare for the RN examination. She failed her first attempt. To improve her chance of passing the examination, she enrolled in a refresher/upgrading program at Lakeview Community College with Nancy as her teacher.

Ana told us she liked being in Nancy's class. She found Nancy to be very friendly, and to have a gift of encouraging students and explaining her materials very clearly. Ana found, however, that teaching techniques were different in Canada. The system used in the refresher/upgrading program required students to prepare ahead of time, but Ana had little time to prepare for class. With long hours of working, she missed classes, was late in handing in assignments, and could not find enough time to study for the RN examination.

After the coffee break, Nancy put up an overhead with a list of four teaching principles:

1. Activities should enhance the learners' abilities
2. Good rapport between teacher and learner
3. Use of previous learning
4. Clear and concise communication

Nancy said that teaching principles and learning principles were intertwined. She asked the students to think about teachers who had an impact on them. Some students yelled out answers at random: "Equal relationship between student and teacher." "Somebody who smiles a lot." Nancy asked, "Do you mean somebody who enjoys teaching?" The responses came: "Someone who has something relevant to say." "Someone who is knowledgeable." "Someone who is fairly objective, not opinionated." "Somebody who understands our needs." "Somebody who has respect. Sorry, I mean there should be respect between students and teacher." "The teacher should have a sense of humor." Nancy copied the answers on the board. Another student said, "A good teacher is like a friend." Nancy explained: "This belongs to equal relationship." One student told a story to illustrate what she meant by trust in teaching. Some students mentioned dealing with their patients. Nancy replied, "Ah, that belongs to communication skills." She mentioned verbal and nonverbal skills.

Nancy began to talk about pedagogy and androgogy. She had an overhead about pedagogy and a list of five assumptions underlying androgogy:

1. Moving from dependency to self-directedness
2. Accumulated experience
3. Readiness to learn
4. Immediate application
5. Problem-centered learning

Students copied notes from the overhead. Sometimes if they could not copy quickly enough, they turned to copy from their neighbor's notebook.

Nancy connected teaching and learning principles to the care of patients. She adapted Elizabeth Kubler Ross's five stages of grieving about death and dying to five stages of illness. As she explained what each of these stages meant, she asked the students what stage would be appropriate for teaching to take place. The students felt that bargaining and acceptance were natural stages in which to teach patients, since the other stages would not be appropriate, when the patients are either denying, angry, or depressed. She illustrated teaching procedures on another overhead:

1. Take control of learning environment
2. Find out what your patients already know
3. Tell your patients what you will teach and why
4. Stress the patients' learning responsibility
5. Present your message clearly and enthusiastically
6. Use approved teaching aids
7. Summarize important points
8. Ask questions and wait for answers
9. Provide feedback

She encouraged students to review what had been covered in the class. "This content," she explained, "was on the previous RN exam. It could appear in the upcoming midterm exam as well as in the RN exam!"

In later interviews and conversations, we asked Nancy to share her thoughts and feelings about her class, which she did:

> I think that small-group discussions are wonderful if you have a small class. And, also, when you've got time. I've always envied teachers that had an entire semester to teach one topic. I don't have that luxury. And I've got a group of students who are also not used to that format. What I found with this group—unless there's someone in the group who takes leadership, they don't get anything done. Because they don't know how to use their time in small groups. They're coming to me from learning environments where they sat in rows, and the teacher told them what they had to know, and they didn't have the luxury of thinking for themselves. (Field notes, November 14, 1995)

Nancy elaborated that her way of teaching was perhaps connected with her education, her practice, and her teaching experiences. As a student in the early 1970s, she disliked her psychiatric training. Her teacher "hated psychiatry" and "did not want to teach the subject." She gradually came to hold the same view as her teacher, although her highest mark on the RN examination was in psychiatry. Reflecting on her psychiatric experiences as a student, she realized that she had disliked the theoretical component but had enjoyed working with psychiatric patients. Nancy remembered that she had

always wanted to make a contribution to psychiatric nursing. After graduation, however, she could not find a psychiatric nursing job in the city. She
moved to the Maritimes and worked in an orthopedic unit. She returned to
the city a year later and worked in a general surgical unit in a large hospital.
She struggled to fit into this new environment. Eventually she decided to leave
nursing:

> I really hated it. It was very short staffed. I used to work nights, by myself,
> with no help at all. I mean, there were no aides, nobody. There was just me
> and the 22 post-op patients. I did not like what I was doing. I felt that I didn't
> give enough to my patients. . . . One of the feelings that I had when I was doing
> surgical nursing was that I could not talk to the patients. I would see the fear
> in them of going into surgery, and the anxiety about being in a hospital. I did
> not have 5 extra minutes to sit down with them. At that point, I decided to get
> out of nursing altogether. I did my degree in psychology. . . . But then I missed
> nursing. (Conversation, March 28, 1995)

Nancy attempted to move out of nursing, but she missed the practice.
She wanted to return to it in a different capacity from bedside nursing. She
did psychiatric crisis and emergency nursing in a mental hospital for
2 years. Then she decided to work in the Caribbean as a nurse on a ship.
She began to appreciate the connection between the nurse and the educator. Nancy decided to obtain her university degree in nursing. She encountered difficulty, however, in getting into the nursing degree program because
she did not have Grade 13 English and chemistry credits. At 27 she returned
to high school during the day and worked as a nurse in the evening. She
resented having to do these high school courses. She felt that she had ex-
tensive work experience and a university degree in psychology, but these
were not enough.

> I did a degree at the university in nursing. It was one of the most horrible
> experiences of my life. I do believe that my experiences in my education have
> a great influence on my teaching students. I hated my nursing experience at
> the university. They treated me like I had no brains at all. We were told that,
> "you know, your [college] diploma does not mean much. You were taught
> wrong the first time, we can't undo what they have already done. You will
> never get an A." It was very demoralizing. (Conversation, March 28, 1995)

However, Nancy still had a strong passion for nursing:

> I like nursing! I wanted to instill a love of nursing into my students without
> them hating the educational process. So, I try and talk to them about, you know,
> this is what we're supposed to do, but this is the reality. This is what really

happens out there and this is how you can deal with it. I use a lot of anecdotal-type stuff in class, a lot of it. And sometimes the students like that; sometimes they don't. I've had feedback in both ways. More often, I have students come back to me and say, "You know, when I was writing the RN exam, I could hear you telling me about that patient you had." Because we remember patients we've taken care of. So I use a lot of anecdotal stuff to help them hold on to something, but not just to write the exams. I try to reinforce what is important about being a nurse. We did "Death and Dying" and it's a really difficult topic. How do you deal with dying patients? How do you deal with families of dying patients? And I mean, I talk to them about, "It's okay to sit and cry with them. It's okay to sit and hug them. There's nothing wrong with that. It's okay to say, "I don't know where we go from here." So, I try and instill a little bit more of the humanities, instead of making it all clinical. (Conversation, November 14, 1995)

Nancy's teaching had to keep pace with dramatic changes from policies, students, budget cuts, and society. Transfer grants for education from the federal to the provincial government decreased. Community colleges had to create new avenues to get more funding. Nancy's community college was developing international marketing strategies to recruit students from foreign countries. Her class size had become larger because the institution had to accept more students to increase revenue. However, the increasing number of nursing students prepared for the job market did not match the decreasing number of nursing positions in Canada.

Nancy was experiencing dramatic changes in her institution, which added to the complexity of her teaching. She maintained a constant resistance to the way she was educated, in which teachers lectured and students received knowledge. She told us that she wanted her students to have a different kind of education, one that was more personal and that involved more sharing of experiences. She wanted to "instill a love of nursing" in her students through her teaching. However, she was driven to deliver knowledge in a lecture format in which her students had to hurry through preparation for the RN exam. Nancy had a tremendous theoretical understanding of teaching and learning principles. She tried to bring in her own clinical experience into her classroom teaching. She said: "Unfortunately, I have a lot of curriculum to cover in a very short time."

Nancy lived a story of cultural complexity brought into her classroom by students. The diversity of her students' cultural, educational, and language backgrounds was filtered into her classroom through the institutional education system, Nancy's past and present experiences, and her students' past experiences and present expectations to pass the RN exam. She had to design the curriculum and deliver as much content as possible to students in order to enable them to pass the RN exam while these students were going through a flux of changes in their personal and professional lives. The RN exam did not include the previous knowledge and experience of this diverse group. As Ana said, the exam was mainly designed for Canadian-born students, not for "a multicultural population with different religious backgrounds, different family orientations, different traditions and practices." Although these students passed the exam, it was not always possible for them to get nursing positions. Positioning Nancy's story of teaching in the landscape she was living, we found that the nursing landscape was dramatically changing due to economic and social changes in society. And while the landscape itself was changing, the stories in this landscape were also evolving. How will these changes continue to affect Nancy's story of teaching?

CHAPTER 5

Shaping Sara's Practice

Chuck Rose

In the fall of 1990, two days prior to the opening of school, Sara came to Briardon Junior High, where I was principal. She was seeking her first teaching position and was recommended for an interview by the recruitment officer responsible for screening new applicants. I walked across the floor of the main office to greet her and escorted her into the principal's office, where I invited her to be seated on one of the comfortable chairs. To facilitate conversation and to ease her nervousness, I avoided the chair behind the desk and sat beside her on another chair.

I found myself reflecting on my initial observations as we eased into our discussion. For example, I could not help but notice how young she appeared. It occurred to me that if not for the professional manner in which she was attired, she might easily be taken for one of the students. She was a lot like them. Her sandy colored hair was straight and shoulder length. It framed her face and highlighted the unmistakable signs of youth—freckles. They dotted her summer-tanned face, particularly her nose and the upper portion of her cheeks. I wondered how this soft-spoken and almost timid young woman might fare among Grade 8 and 9 students, many of whom were noticeable by their size, gregariousness, and often intimidating personas.

Any doubts I had were quickly chased away as we began our discussion. I mispronounced her last name. She corrected me and I apologized. She waved off my apology, putting me at ease by telling me that it happened frequently. In that brief exchange I recognized, in her quiet and matter-of-fact handling of the matter, a confidence and selflessness I would later come to appreciate as one of her many strengths. Although she had cause to expect that I would know her name from my discussion with the recruitment officer, she did not take offense at my error. Instead she responded by helping me.

I was also taken with the warmth of her smile and the confidence embodied in her ability to establish and maintain eye contact with me. That in itself seemed to transform the interview from the thrust and parry of question and answer to open conversation in which she related those things she felt comfortable in sharing.

Three things seemed to stand out in the interview. First, she was very quiet. I found myself conversing with her to find out more about her philosophy and her personal views. I began to appreciate the sense of family she carried and the extent to which stories of teaching were already a part of her knowing. Second, she displayed an unusually strong sense of care and concern for students. Because she responded to the situations and stories I presented with concern for the needs of the students rather than for her own needs, I interpreted her as being "student-centered." Finally, she questioned neither the grade levels, load, complexity, nor extracurricular activities that were part of the assignment. I found her willingness to work with students and her enthusiasm refreshing.

As the discussion drew to a close, I began to feel uncomfortable about the task I was assigning her. The only job available was a half-time position that featured a very fragmented timetable. It was a difficult assignment in which she was required to teach a number of different subjects at different grade levels. She would have to teach some mornings and different afternoons, a feat I recognized from past experience as demanding full-time attention for part-time pay. Although she was eager to accept the job as it was, I found myself promising to do my best to raise the position to full time. While the level of complexity would not be lessened, at least she would be a full-time teacher. She would also know that I supported her.

I recommended that she be hired and, in discussion with superintendents, managed to convince them of the need to make the position full time. By the end of the day I was able to telephone her to let her know of the change, to offer her the job and to welcome her to Briardon. She responded with enthusiasm and excitement and I concluded the call by spending a few minutes outlining events, meeting dates, and times in preparation for the opening that would soon be upon us. As I returned the telephone receiver to its cradle, I began to reflect on Sara's enthusiasm and excitement in light of my knowledge of how difficult it was to teach at this school. My mind wandered back 3 years, to my return to the school system and how my enthusiasm was dampened when I learned of my appointment to Briardon Junior High.

In the fall of 1988, I returned to my practice as a principal after a sabbatical leave to complete a master of arts degree. Initially, I was excited about my return. I was confident that as a result of my study and inquiry, I would find myself more reflective and sensitive to the differing ways in which students and teachers hold and express their personal practical knowledge. I

felt that I understood better that such knowledge is embodied in their practices and was looking forward to a placement in which I would have an
opportunity to draw upon my new learnings. When I received the telephone
call notifying me that I was appointed to Briardon, my enthusiasm waned.

Briardon was known as a difficult school. It was large and complex. Its
reputation for toughness and violence seemed to require a strong focus on
"management" and a high tolerance for the unpredictable. If the assignment
was the luck of the draw, it seemed unjust. Unlike the rodeo cowboy whose
draw carries the potential for reward based on its degree of difficulty, this
assignment promised only a high level of stress and the premature graying
of hair that seemed to have befallen my predecessor.

When I arrived at the school I found a student body numbering about
750 ranging in age from 11 to 17 years. From diverse cultural backgrounds,
a large number of them spoke English as a second language, and approximately 100 had been placed in special education classes. A majority of the
students were storied as unsuccessful—in school and in life generally. Many
came from difficult economic and social circumstances.

Later, I discovered that they could be viewed in a totally different light.
They were open and honest. That is to say that they had a tendency to "tell
it the way they see it"—even if "it" was often expressed in the vernacular of
the street culture. They were inquisitive and would work to prove a point or
to acquire what they wanted. They were willing to question and experiment.
They lived in both mainstream and adolescent worlds. They were survivors.
My story had a different plot line from one of lack of success.

These students responded to loyalty with loyalty. And they were impres-
sionable. With consistency from adults, they could be opened to change. The
following story records an incident in which my story about our students
began to change:

> My first September in the school was hectic. There were a large
> number of teachers, many of them new to teaching. . . . a large
> support and caretaking staff and many, many students. . . . faces to
> remember, names to learn, a plethora of cultures and ethnic back-
> grounds requiring new learnings on my part. As part of the opening
> agenda for the term, I attempted to schedule a school assembly. The
> effort was resisted. Teachers advised that "we don't have total-school
> assemblies here." Large gatherings were too hard to control.
>
> My need to communicate with the students was strong and so I
> offered teachers a free period at the end of the day. After escorting
> their students to the main gym, teachers were given the option to use
> the period for other preparations. Should they prefer, they might go
> home early.

Some of the newer teachers stayed but the majority wanted no part of what they thought would be a control and management nightmare. And, I must admit, it was not easy to acquire and maintain the attention of some 750 teenage people. On the other hand, as the dialogue progressed, more and more students spoke and more and more students listened . . . to me and to each other.

I began by trying to assure them that their administration and teaching staff truly cared about them and wanted to make the year successful, rewarding, and pleasant. I told them that some of our concerns centered upon student deportment and the apparent lack of respect and care for our building and equipment, both inside and out.

One of my suggestions dealt with ways in which we might enhance the quality of our life in the school by painting the place. The walls and ceilings were particularly scarred and worn.

One student mumbled rather loudly. I asked the audience to hear out the classmate. His statement was significant. He asked why students had to obtain their food from a small, corral-like, hole-in-the-wall on the stage, carry it down to the gym floor without spilling it and then eat on the floor while teachers enjoyed relative luxury in the staff room. He continued. "Why are we required to eat on the gym floor or on bleachers and benches? If you really want to help us, then get us a real lunchroom!"

In a flash I understood. And 6 weeks of frustration were drawn forth and focused by this student's questions. I had found it depressing trying to work in the confines of a dilapidated building and with those teachers who seemed to have lost hope or had become hardened and resistant to change. And, in the short time that I had been principal there, I had already added to a stack of requests for repair and refurbishing that had been ignored for years.

Here was an opportunity to unite everyone. Why not do both—build a cafeteria and paint the school? Great solution, but how were we to do it? In front of the students, I was affected, as the problem weighed on me.

I invited any and all who would like to help to meet me after school in the three rooms across from the gym. There we would knock out the cinder-block walls and create our own lunchroom. In my last school, those three rooms had been converted into a lunchroom. That would serve as our model. With the help of caretakers, teachers with home improvement experience, and volunteer parents, we could address the problem ourselves.

The project received great response and started off very well. Everyone was excited and there was an air of anticipation. All work came to an abrupt halt, however, when we discovered that the wiring and piping for the three rooms had been constructed within the walls. It took only a matter of hours for school building officials to arrive.

A few days later I found myself required to account for my actions before a superintendent and provincial building inspector. Armed with my stack of neglected requests for repair, my best argument—"on behalf of our students"—and relying heavily on the good will and student focus of those officials, I explained the history of the school, as I understood it, toured the school with them and offered my plan of hope for the future.

The result drew cheers from our students when, the following day, I informed them that in return for our promise to refrain from such school improvement projects in the future, system workers would finish the removal of the walls, wiring, and piping. We would then get along in that space until the fall, when a new facility would be constructed. It would be completed by Christmas. More good news—some of the school would be painted.

This was a story of my beginning. It was a story about the establishment of trust and the emergence of a relationship that began by my listening and responding to student voice. More than that, it embodied significant changes, change in my story of these students and change in my understanding of what would be needed to transform the school. Two years later Sara came to Briardon.

Shaped in Relationships

Over the course of Sara's first year of teaching, 1990–1991, she lived her teacher stories within a traditional classroom setting that was her in-classroom place. She worked, with dedication, for long hours and many weekends to ensure that her students received the best she could give them. Cooperative learning seemed to fit her ways of teaching and she quickly became successful in working with students using those methods. Like other teachers, she worked, for the most part, in isolation from other professionals.

On the out-of-classroom place she fulfilled her responsibilities for hallway supervision alone, said little in staff meetings, and only on occasion visited the staff room. As the year progressed, however, she became acquainted with the teachers who worked next to her classroom. Through conversations that were a part of visits to their in-classroom place and through inclusion in some of their social activities, she developed a relationship with one of them. She also grew comfortable enough to visit and talk with me in my office. From those conversations our relationship grew.

As she storied it later, these were two locations and two people with whom she found it safe to share her teacher stories. First, she told of becoming aware of an alternative teacher story that was being constructed and lived out in the double-station classroom next door. She shared that story in a journal entry.

> I remember being in the classroom next door to Clark, John and Kay and initially being curious and eventually envious of their "learning community."
> I was envious of their relationships with one another. They laughed, argued, debated, socialized, questioned and always respected each other. I was intrigued by the way they designed their interdisciplinary curriculum. Most of all, I wished for the depth of relationships they had with the young people in their community.

In a second story of relationship, Sara storied me and the principal's office as safe and supportive. She told a story that she described as "a telling one, of a safe place outside of the big room." It was a story about a day in which she experienced some personal difficulty and I responded with support.

Sara's interest in the story being lived by Clark, John, and Kay caused me to reflect on my relationships with them and the history behind the story they were constructing. Once again I found myself transported back to the time of my appointment to Briardon, to those early days, the beginning of my story at the school.

When I arrived at Briardon, I found that some teachers had worked only in that school and for considerable time. Others did not wish to be there and were planning to transfer. A number of them appeared callous and cynical. Still others demonstrated the enthusiasm that characterizes teachers entering the profession. As in other schools serving "high needs" communities, there seemed to be a significant staff turnover at Briardon every year, and beginning teachers were faced with challenges in their first years of teaching that more experienced teachers avoided. In a story that seemed to repeat itself year after year, school opening would arrive and Briardon's staff complement would be short of the number of teachers allocated. Because of transfers, resignations, or fluctuations in student numbers, the staffing was never addressed by the end of the term nor over the summer. Sometimes it was completed the day prior to opening and, at other times, after school had begun.

As principal, I found it frustrating that staffing interfered with school-opening preparations. On the other hand, there was a silver lining to the problem. Beginning teachers brought a freshness, new ideas and the potential for change. Like a prospector mining uncharted ground, I approached my interviews with beginning teachers looking for signs of richness and filled with hope.

Like Sara would be 2 years later, Clark was one of those beginning teachers. He began his teaching career the same year I came to the school. In the interview from which I recommended his hiring, he demonstrated exceptional insight and perspective. His belief in the potential of students and in their need for voice in their learning and his focus on relationships resonated with me. He was one of two new teachers who accepted my opening staff meeting invitation to begin a journaling relationship. We maintained our journaling for the full year, after which he asked me to participate in a yearlong administrative practicum, part of the requirements for his university master's program. It was through the dialogue and discussion that were a part of those undertakings that we developed a strong and close relationship.

By the end of my first year in Briardon, I had not only changed my views with respect to our students, but I was determined to recruit teachers whose teacher stories featured an understanding of relationship as central to student learning. John was an experienced teacher who was particularly well-suited to the school by virtue of his easy-going manner and his proven ability to initiate and maintain positive relationships with difficult students. He was a teacher-leader with whom I had worked in two previous school settings. It was John's talent in relating with students, along with my need for positive relationships with teachers, that found me inviting him to the school.

Clark found it easy to talk to John. In safe locations on the out-of-classroom place on the landscape, the two of them shared secret stories of their practices and explored the potential of future stories. Near the end of that year, they responded to my invitation for teachers to rethink the way in which they viewed our students and to restory their practices. They put forth the idea that they be given a group of students for whom they would be totally responsible. That is, they would depart from the traditional specialized subject-content approach and, instead, construct a new teacher story based on close relationships with students. They would teach all of the core subjects.

I shaped their story somewhat by suggesting that they involve a third teacher, Kay, who, some years earlier, taught in an elementary "open-area school" that featured team teaching. I was her principal then and my assignment to Briardon coincided with her return to teaching after a 12-year leave to raise her children. Like John, she agreed to an appointment at Briardon and we renewed our relationship.

Thus, as Sara was beginning her first year of teaching, Clark, John, and Kay began to experiment with notions of community in teaching, intent on constructing an alternative teacher story. In her visits to their in-classroom place, Sara viewed this alternative story being lived out, rethought, restoried, and relived. Although she worked in relative isolation in her own in-classroom place, she also began to live out a very different teacher story than was lived by most other teachers at the school.

In safe locations on the out-of-classroom place, she shared her stories with Clark and she heard his stories. In this way, they developed a relationship in which it was safe to explore their practices. Over the course of the term and within the security of her relationships with Clark and with John and Kay, she found support. Like them, she was able to shape the context of her own in-classroom place and resist shaping influences from other teachers living out a story of school that did not fit with hers.

Over the course of one year, our relationship also grew. It became one of trust and mutual support. She felt confident in sharing her teacher stories with me and shared the story she was attempting to construct and live out with her students. She accepted my support, encouragement, and, at times, a suggestion or two.

Shaping the Context of Sara's In-Classroom Place

The context of Sara's work was shaped in other ways during her first year. It was shaped in the fall from the out-of-classroom place by the violence issue that engulfed the school with interruptions to daily rhythms, threats to safety and security and a story of school that again portrayed Briardon as a difficult and violent place. It was also shaped by events on the in-classroom place as the violence issue gave way to a new story of school.

Several students asked to be allowed to share the results of their research into the problem of violence in and around the school and community. In the alternative story that Clark, John, and Kay were constructing with their 105 students, the notion of community became a theme of study and the violence issue, an opportunity for inquiry. Personal experience was the starting point for student research. Students questioned, researched and then presented and supported their arguments to other students, teachers, and, finally, to the adults who attended an open forum.

Sara participated in that forum and liked what she saw. Three things apparent in the story lived by those three teachers were also part of the story she was living with her students. First, the view of students held by teachers was one in which students were viewed as already having knowledge. Second, the students were given voice, an opportunity to express their knowledge, to share their personal experience, to learn from others, and to take part in the dialogue. Finally, the students questioned and were encouraged to question. In this way, the curriculum took on a new relevance and personal meaning. The students had an influence on their community. They became authors of the story they would live out in their school and community. In the context of the violence issue, the shaping of another powerful influence was resisted. Clark, John, Kay, and—by virtue of the story she was constructing—Sara began to shape the context of the school and the community from their in-classroom places on the landscape.

As principal, I was influenced and shaped. The quality of the students' presentations, the research done by them, and the progress that appeared evident by way of improved student attitudes and relationships within their new "learning community," drew me closer to the teacher stories being lived by the three of them and by Sara. As a result, and through the school leadership team, a new story of school was presented to the staff and accepted. The new story of school was one of five learning communities, each empowered to develop its own plot lines and to live out those stories with its students.

In this new plot line, the story lived by Clark, John, and Kay would be supported, Sara's story would be supported, those who followed the dominant story could continue to live out their story, and there would be support for those who might live other different stories. Learning communities became a school story and the context of the out-of-classroom place was again shaped, this time by the practices of teachers working on their in-classroom places.

Shaped by Conflicting Teacher Stories

In preparation for the new school story that would be lived over the course of the 1991–1992 school term, teachers formed their own teacher teams and started to organize, structure timetables and negotiate what was needed to live out their teacher stories with their students. Inspired by their relationship of the previous year, Sara joined Clark's team. John and Kay became leaders of their own learning communities.

In that way Sara began her 2nd year of teaching in a different context. It was one in which she worked closely with her team leader, Clark, as they and four other teachers began to organize, structure, and live out their teacher stories within a story of school that saw the learning community as a "democratic community of learners working cooperatively to grow and to develop."

As they began to integrate curriculum and explore team-teaching and cooperative learning methods, Sara and Clark realized that their teacher stories were in competition with the stories of the other four teachers, part of their team, who did not feel comfortable living that teacher story. Before long, the competing stories became conflicting ones. Sara and Clark found themselves occupying the team-teaching room, where, together, they attempted to live out their alternative story of teaching with some of the students. The other teachers moved into individual classrooms with other students to live out the story that was once dominant in the school. Theirs was a story of teachers as specialists. It was the way they knew their practices and was the way they knew school.

For the remainder of that term, Sara, Clark, and the others lived out a cover story that all was well. That is they lived it until I discovered conflict on the in-classroom place and, at the end of the year, facilitated moves for the teachers who wanted out and replaced them with teachers who wanted to live the learning community story initially lived by Sara and Clark. By means of teachers transferring to Briardon and new hirings in which Clark was involved, a new team was formed and the learning community context was restoried with teachers who wanted to live the story that focused on relationships with students and that featured cooperative learning, integrated curriculum, and team-teaching methods.

Restorying the Context for Success

From the start of Sara's 3rd year of teaching, greater attention was given to relationships and to the teacher stories each person brought to the context of the new team. For example, every Friday afternoon the team would gather in their team-teaching area. They would relax in the reading corner and tell stories. They would talk about students, how things were going in the unit, where they were going and what they were doing. Every week they revisited some of their beliefs.

In one of the stories Sara shared with me, she described the context of the restoried in-classroom place and the openness and security that this area provided for her and the team.

> The "big room," our triple-sized classroom, is the heart of our school wing in much the same way as the kitchen is often the heart of a family home. It is the first place teachers and students go in the morning to talk over coffee and breakfast. The big room even has a fridge, microwave, kettle, and toaster for anyone to cook up what they would like.
>
> There are six teachers who share this school wing and we team-teach our 150 or so students. The big room contains all our desks and many tables and chairs, is fully carpeted, and has a corner with comfortable couches and chairs.
>
> The couch area has been dubbed the "relaxation zone." This is where we sit with the students, in the morning and at lunch, to just talk about our lives. It is also a place where we most often meet with

our student "ministers," to talk about ways of improving, changing, and shaping the work we do together.

During our common preparation time, we all gravitate to the "relaxation zone" to consider the days behind and ahead of us. We talk about our successes and the concerns and ask ourselves why certain approaches worked while others did not. We share conversations we have had with our students, parents, and colleagues and wonder what our responses should be. It is a safe place to agree, disagree, argue, debate, question, dream, and wonder.

When the six team members decided to go to Sara's lakeside cabin for a weekend planning session, they intended to plan a unit of study. However, according to how Sara told this story, other things happened.

It was a mid-October Friday evening when we arrived at the cabin. We decided to make a nice dinner and retire early so as to be as productive as possible the next day.

Bernie, a teacher new to our school, with a traditional language arts background, was up the earliest and was outside watching the birds and appreciating nature.

When everyone was awake and stuffed with a cholesterol-laden breakfast, we sat down to plan our Consumer Product Testing Unit. We were trying to balance the curriculum requirements in the different subject areas, address the role of the student in making curricular decisions, and consider all of our ideas on the best approach. A lot of time was spent revisiting our beliefs about students, teaching, learning, knowledge, schools, and our philosophy so that whatever we decided upon, it was based firmly on our values and beliefs about what is best for students.

After about 3 hours we had worked out a general idea of how the unit was going to "look" but had not begun to hash out any details. It was at this point that Bernie shocked us all.

(In order for anyone who does not know Bernie to appreciate our reaction, a bit of background is required. He is a religious man, very caring, considerate, and positive. At least this was my impression of him after almost 2 months of working together.)

He interrupted what we were discussing about the unit and blurted out, "I haven't spent so much #*!$^*@ time planning in 15 years! When the #*$@ are we going to have lunch?"

We all stared at him in disbelief. I don't think any of us had heard him swear at all before, much less twice in one statement! We all laughed and took a break for lunch.

That evening, when the unit was as prepared as it was going to get, we spent some time debating life's more important issues. Who were better, the Beatles or the Rolling Stones? Should Clark name his first born Kent? What are all the words to the Brady Bunch theme song? Which is better for you, beer or red wine?

Back at school on Monday, we all felt we knew each other just a little bit better and felt closer together. More than anything else though, I had just begun to realize what a special part of our team Bernie was going to be. He has a lot of experience in education that is invaluable, but is also willing to try something completely new and foreign to him. He kept us rooted in reality without discouraging what we were trying to do and he did everything with a great sense of humor.

At the end of the year Bernie said something that I have carried around with me ever since: "At the beginning of the year I didn't know what to expect and I was leery as to how it would work out. Now I look back on this year and think it was one of the greatest years of teaching in my career. I feel revitalized!"

The team developed a sense of appreciation and caring for one another. The cabin provided a safe spot on the out-of-classroom place on the landscape for Sara and her colleagues. Positive relationships prevailed throughout the year and, as a result, Sara storied the 1992–1993 school term as a satisfying and successful year for and with the four new teachers and 150 students for whom that learning community was home.

As that year progressed, different versions of our school story became known on the landscape. Responding to requests to speak about the school violence issue and how we were coping at Briardon, I began to tell my new story of school at principals' meetings, with the media, at seminars, and at educational conferences. Teacher-leaders told their stories of school in their knowledge communities and in places that were safe for them. And those who were responsible for supervising Briardon began to tell different stories of school on the landscape. It was not long before visitors from other schools and other school systems came to Briardon to observe the transformation and to interact with us.

When I was invited to speak about the violence issue, I was able to tell a story of school that featured teachers transforming education with their students and constructing and living out unique and different stories of school within the same building. At some of the conferences outside of our school system, learning community teacher-leaders accompanied me and helped me tell our story of school. A number of those presentations found Clark, Sara, and me presenting our story of transformation collaboratively. Before long

Sara and Clark were sharing their learning community story at school professional days and at conferences.

As principal, I knew that the restorying of Sara and Clark's learning community was necessary if the fulfillment of their story was to be facilitated. Through the stories Sara and Clark shared with me, I was aware of the success they were living in their wing of the school throughout the 1992–1993 school term. I was even aware of their meetings on out-of-classroom places in the evenings, on weekends at the university, at each others' homes, at social events, and at Sara's cabin. But I was not privileged to the depth and richness of detail of, and what was embodied in, the stories they told. Nor could I appreciate the connections between events, experiences, and what I saw in their practices; that is, until my transition from principal to researcher. My story of visiting Sara at her cabin explains how I began to understand Sara's practice much differently as a researcher when I returned to university the year following our school transformation.

> On one of my return trips home from the university in the fall of 1993, I visited Sara at her lakeside cabin to talk about the possibility of conducting my research with her. It was overcast, bordering on rain, and there was a strong breeze. She greeted me at the door.
>
> Inside, she introduced me to her aunt who, with a friend, was assembling a puzzle. Her brother, Marc, also had a friend visiting. As I remember it, Marc and his friend were immersed in some activity and the radio was playing. The cabin looked lived in and seemed to be a place to relax. The decor was casual and informal. The feeling was warm and hospitable. It was accepting.
>
> Everyone greeted me and then returned to what they had been doing. Sara took me out back, through the property, along the lakefront and around the perimeter of cabins that made up the community. We then returned through the driveway by which the residents entered their cabins. In that way she showed me around and shared some of the community with me.
>
> We talked about the possibilities provided by the research and I asked her to consider participating with me.
>
> In the short time I was there, and especially inside the cabin, I was taken by the unquestioned acceptance and the sense of warmth and belonging that seemed to permeate the place. It was as though I had been accepted as part of the family.

For a fleeting moment during that visit, it occurred to me that Sara's team-teaching area resembled her cabin. As I began to work with her and her team in my new capacity as a participant-observer researcher, I made similar connections. In one instance I visited her at her home and I again met Marc and was introduced to her mother and father. Then and since, when I have spoken with them by phone or at their home, they have been warm, friendly, and welcoming. Again I sensed a special kind of caring. In a second situation I met with Sara and her team in a summer planning meeting. The meeting was at her house; the atmosphere was noticeably relaxed and informal. As at the cabin, the important thing seemed to be the people rather than the organization of the house or the preparation for the meeting. It was welcoming. There was care and acceptance. By then I could make the connection. That same atmosphere was embodied in Sara's team-teaching area. Although I had been in the "big room" many times in my capacity as principal, I had not been able to appreciate the connections between home, cabin, and teaching. My participant-observer account of her team-teaching room will serve to illustrate.

The former elementary library is affectionately called "the big room." It serves as a general gathering place for the entire learning community. It is open and available before school, at noon, and after school hours. Students come early, check in, eat lunch, and spend the noon hour and after-school times here. Students are allowed to come and go, wear their baseball caps and just hang out. Surprisingly, many do homework, and not surprisingly, other students drop by. This includes high school students who were in this learning community in previous years.

There are always teachers here. They eat lunch with the students and rarely frequent the staff room when they could be with students. When the entire learning community meets, it is in this room. It is very crowded. For the most part, however, some 60–90 students are accommodated at any given time.

The "big room" looks lived in. More precisely, it is a little old and worn. It has not been painted for many years. The wood finish on the doors has been chipped and marked, as have the table tops. When preparing to make the transition to the five learning communities, tubular desks and individual flattop tables were abandoned in favor of larger tables that would facilitate cooperative activities and group work. In order to obtain enough of those tables, a great deal of "scrounging" occurred and the end result was the acceptance of some very ancient and poorly finished wooden tables. The pen and pencil markings that have accumulated on these items over time contribute to the well-used look of the place.

At the west end of the big room, a small library office serves as a general work and storage room. It holds a refrigerator that is accessible to anyone in the learning community. In the mornings, toast and hot chocolate are served to those who are hungry and both students and teachers share their lunches with others. Given the general access to this small room by so many people, it can be understood why it looks lived in.

The remainder of the west end serves as a reading corner. It is bordered by windows and is replete with risers, two old chesterfields, and some easy chairs. Be it seat work, class discussion time, or direct teaching, there are always students who rush to these choice areas to lounge or do their work in a more relaxed fashion. Those who don't get seated on the old chesterfields or on the reading-corner risers often make themselves at home on the floor. The floor area is carpeted, the covering having been donated by an oil company. The installation was done by parents.

Teacher desks are clustered around the big room, some of them side by side and others separate. The majority of the room is filled with the old tables and auditorium chairs. Simply put, the big room does not look neat and tidy. But teachers and students don't seem to mind. The people seem to be the focus.

There is always lots of chatter and it seems like a happy and positive place to be.

The atmosphere at Sara's home, at her cabin, and in the learning community seemed connected. It was relaxed, it was warm. Everyone was accepted and welcomed. No one was turned away. It was like family.

A New Story Shapes Sara's Practice

When I decided to return to university at the end of the 1992–1993 school term, the superintendent arranged for Clark to transfer and, after only 3 years of teaching, Sara was invited to become a teacher-leader. She anticipated that she would coordinate the team as they continued to live out their teacher stories within the story of school she initially helped shape, a story of school that supported and encouraged competing teacher stories. But things did not unfold as she anticipated. Relationships shifted and a different story emerged with the new principal. From his opening address and from conversations she had with him during the fall, Sara became aware that he wanted a different story of school. He was concerned that competing stories were being lived in the school. Rather than unique stories of school within each learning community, he wanted a common story across the learning communities. The plot line of the new story was to be "harmony among learning groups," the same story of school in each learning community. It was to be a "one vision" story of school.

Sara did not abandon her team's story of school. Over the course of the 1993–1994 school year and into the next, she worked hard to acquire the support of her new principal. In the end, however, her efforts to talk, to relate, to get him to visit her in-classroom place, and to enlist his support for her story were unsuccessful. She felt ambivalent towards him, frustrated and unsupported. Her story, the story of school lived by her team, did not fit with his one-vision story of school. She began to realize that the relationship she once had with the principal, as a safe person on the landscape, had changed. The principal was now situated on the professional knowledge landscape as an unsafe person.

The Dominant Story Permeates Sara's In-Classroom Place

The story of teaching lived in Sara's community was again shaped by unexpected changes. In planning for 1993–1994, teachers in the school agreed to advance to the next grades along with their students. Yet, in their planning for the subsequent term, and after their trying it for only one year, the practice was abandoned. Sara, her team, and others who supported the practice were out voted. The success of their students from 1992–1993 to 1993–1994 convinced them that 3 years in a learning community with the same teachers were needed to ensure a successful junior high experience. On the other hand, teachers in other communities grew tired of working with the same students. Some students were perceived to be very difficult to manage and their teachers wanted a change.

Therefore, instead of beginning the 1994–1995 year with a learning community of new Grade 7s whom they would teach for 3 years, Sara's team was assigned a group of students who had been in another community for the previous 2 years. The group included mainstream Grade-9 students, students labeled English as a second language and special education, and a group in a "special program" category whose program needs were addressed with a staff allocation of two teachers rather than one. Given the story lived in her learning community, by all of the teachers and students, it was assumed that subject matter would be integrated and that her team would be able to work with students of such varying abilities.

But the year began with about 180 students in her community, 30 more than projected. It quickly became difficult for Sara and her teachers to work in co-operative groups in the way in which they had been accustomed. The principal asked her to be patient until "adjustments" could be made. As they awaited the addition of two teachers, Sara and her team began to work with their new students to develop relationships and to develop the sense of community around which their story of a "democratic community of learners" would continue to be lived. Instead of the traditional orientation to the rules and procedures set by the teachers, students were engaged in group work and activities in which they became acquainted and from which they developed a charter of student rights and a set of student responsibilities.

Because the plot line of their alternative story of school was that of working with students throughout the day and in all aspects of the curriculum instead of only in specified subjects, positive relationships and knowledge of their students were the foci of teachers' efforts. A variety of thematic units were planned in which research projects would be undertaken. "Skill building" classes would support those units through instruction on specific skills.

Because their story also called for an alternative to the hierarchical basis of power and control from which teachers traditionally practiced, they dressed casually and invited the students to call them by first name. And teachers did not "hassle" students who wore baseball caps or leather jackets or baggy pants. In addition, the big room was again open and accessible to students for lunch, after school, and in the morning before classes. Some students brought lunch from home, others purchased food and beverages from the school cafeteria or from the lunchroom vending machines. Still others brought "slurpees," burgers, or fries from the neighborhood fast food outlets and convenience stores. Food and drink was shared with those who had neither food nor money and, in the morning, prior to school, toast, hot chocolate, and coffee continued to be available to those who were hungry.

As September passed, it became clear that the anticipated adjustments would not be forthcoming. The other learning communities did not wish to give up staff, and teacher-leaders presented a variety of arguments to justify keeping their allocations. Sara explained the way this happened. She described a special meeting called to address the problem.

> A lunchtime administrative team meeting was called near the end of
> September when the enrollment had appeared to stabilize. The
> learning communities still had imbalanced pupil-teacher ratios and
> our team believed we should have at least one, if not two, full-time
> teachers added to our team.
>
> All the other learning community coordinators came well
> prepared and were able to give reasoned and convincing arguments
> for not giving up any of their teachers. It was then suggested that we
> transfer a group of students to another LC with a lower pupil-teacher
> ratio. My colleagues around the table didn't seem to understand that
> this would have been acceptable in the 1st or 2nd week of school, but
> not after the completion of our community unit that emphasized
> inclusiveness, belonging, and student voice and choice. We seemed to

be at an impasse, with people unwilling to move from their bargaining positions. The lunch bell rang and everyone agreed we would have further discussions. I wondered how long we would have to wait for some resolution, and what form that resolution would take. I was frustrated and angry.

The only alternative offered was for Sara and her team to shift some of the students into other learning communities. If the 30 special-program students left the community, there would be no need to provide additional teachers and the learning community numbers would be reduced to the 150, originally agreed upon as acceptable. That presented Sara with a dilemma. Her teaching team was struggling under the load of 180 students, 60 too many, by the special-program formula. But, given the commitment to community that they had established with their students in the first 2 weeks, and now that they had been together nearly a month, they were not prepared to put any of the students out. The care, the voice and choice, and the sense of community would be compromised were any of the students required to leave, now that a sense of community had been established. So Sara waited. And she waited some more. The other teacher-leaders would not give in.

Finally, near the end of September, the administrative team imposed a solution in which Sara's team was loaned the equivalent of one teacher, in the form of different teachers, on a period-by-period basis. It was a story that was remarkably similar to the specialist story once dominant in the school. Fragments of teacher time were available to be redistributed.

The fragmentation that characterized the specialist story was evident in the manner in which the other leaders seemed to feel that Sara had the problem and also in their belief that it could be resolved by loaning her different teachers in different periods, rather than by providing full-time teachers. Like a sacred story (Crites, 1971), it went unquestioned and was assumed to be the only way.

The imposed solution shaped Sara's practice in a number of ways. It forced her and her team back into a story of teacher specialists where some of the students were rotated and scheduled through the teachers assigned to help. Because those teachers were committed to particular subjects and scheduled into this learning community for one period only, they could not spend the time with students in the variety of contexts that were required for teachers to know and relate to them, as called for in the learning community story. Thus the focus on relationship was compromised.

Some students were scheduled with the specialists, whereas the others remained a part of the learning community. In that, the sense of community was also compromised. And teaming was endangered. Teachers scheduled into the learning community for a single period could not fully commit themselves to Sara's team as well as to their own. They could not be available for collaborative team planning, nor could they be available for the ongoing dialogue and professional development that were a part of the everyday work in Sara's team. What was lost was the commitment to the integrated whole upon which the learning community story rested.

Under this new arrangement, Sara's team was still short of the staff enjoyed by the other learning communities. And yet, they found themselves responsible for the care and general well-being of all 180 students, for supervision, preparation, record keeping, and paperwork. It became even more difficult to integrate curriculum, to do co-operative group work, and to have students move from group to group.

Sara's practice was shaped even further. The integrated, interdisciplinary, team-teaching, and cooperative learning aspects of her story were severely constrained as flexibility was lost and control of time was subtly relocated on the out-of-classroom place through a master timetable. This shaping influence was evident in a situation in which the team attempted to readdress the matter of community following a fight in which students from Sara's learning community beat another student.

The teachers undertook special class discussions to involve all students and to revisit their commitments to the dimensions of community that were established by the students at the beginning of the year. The charter of rights and responsibilities were to be discussed as they pertained to the incident and the general caring and support within the community would receive attention and review. In Sara's group, the bell interrupted the discussion at a crucial point. But the school-wide timetable took precedence. To ensure that the specialist teacher met his class as scheduled, the discussion was curtailed before the goals and purposes of the task were realized. Under the story lived by Sara before the imposition of the administrative solution, the bell would have been ignored, the discussion would have continued and curriculum plans would have been adjusted in the following team meeting. Here, the story of school lived on the out-of-classroom place and by the majority of teachers within their in-classroom places permeated Sara's in-classroom place. It shaped her practice and the story of school she earlier helped construct. No longer was her learning community free to teach according to their own teaching stories. No longer did the story of school support competing stories within different learning communities. The new story was a single story of school.

A Story in Conflict

In staff meeting discussions Sara sensed the conflict between the story she and her team were living with their students and the story that was lived by other teachers and dominant on the out-of-classroom part of the land-scape in Briardon. She described one of those discussions as follows:

> Then there was a discussion about how we make decisions . . . what should be the processes. . . . and it was opened up for people to express their opinions . . . it started off quite good, because people were talking in a general sort of way. . . . "the more say you have in decisions, the more you feel responsible for them." . . . Someone on my team said, "Then, we should be involving students."
> And then it got down to things like, "Goddamn it, we need a rule on slurpees and we need to all agree to it!" "Everyone needs to agree to it and then we need to legislate it!" "We need these kids to know it, we need to enforce it and we need to make sure that there are absolute consequences if those rules are broken!" It got down to . . . complaining about different things and wanting those kinds of rules . . . and the word "jail" came up.

Some teachers were upset about the hats, the foodstuff, the slurpees, the use of teachers' first names, and the students' responses to teachers who challenged them on those issues in the hallways and common areas of the school. Others wanted rules that would prevent Sara and her team from allowing students such freedoms in their learning community. They could not perceive the use of teacher first names, the wearing of hats, the food-stuff and drinks, or the questions from students as anything other than dis-regard for the knowledge and authority of teachers. As she reflected upon it, shared the story with Clark and me in our evening meetings, and wrote in her journal, she began to figure out that, for her students, traveling through the out-of-classroom places to the sanctuary of the in-classroom place was not safe.

> Our kids get hit in the main hall, library hall, guidance hall, and then they're safe. . . . it's like monopoly . . . trying to miss the ones with houses.

The story of school lived out by Sara, her teachers, and the students in their learning community contrasted sharply with the traditional story of relationship between students and teachers that was again dominant in the school. Their story was one in which the preferred relationship was one of mutual respect, cooperation, and friendship. It was a relationship in which there was no hierarchy, no difference in status between teacher and student, and in which there was an absence of control over students by virtue of the power of that traditional difference in status. The invitation for students to call teachers by first name embodied the dimensions of that relationship. Those dimensions were also reflected in the relaxed atmosphere of the big room. They were embodied in the unconditional acceptance, welcome, and caring that characterized teacher practice and the approach to discipline that was featured. Students were not sent to the office from this community and students were not "kicked out."

Sara's image of family set a tone that was evident in the openness of the big room, its informality and acceptance. It invited relationship and welcomed students. It accepted the foodstuff and the "hanging out." It was unconditional and devoid of the control and power many of the students had come to associate with school. It was a story that Sara believed in; it was a story that she was prepared to stand up for; it was her story and it was in conflict with the traditional and dominant story in the school.

Sara recognized the way in which the changes and decisions conflicted with and undermined her teacher story and the story of school around which her learning community was constructed. The decisions with respect to the staffing and the teachers' "moving up" with their students, combined with the subtle return to a school-wide timetable, demonstrated the lack of collaborative relationships in the school. Yet, those who lived the specialist story perceived themselves to be collaborative and democratic. They voted on things.

Sara's journal reflections offer further insight into the notions of collaboration embodied in her practice and lived out in her learning community's story. The following excerpt compares what she sees as happening on staff with what happens in her learning community:

> The staff meeting on Wednesday has been on my mind for a few days. . . . some interesting points brought up. . . . stirred some thought, questions, and yes, passion.
>
> Collaboration was a word used in both the handout and during the meeting. My sense was that although we were all using or hearing the word, we didn't share a common meaning. . . . we were referring to collaboration as a "method" or "technique" to make decisions.
>
> For me, collaboration is more. . . . it involves talk about beliefs, understandings, values. . . . a shared language develops. . . . involves sharing a purpose and finding support and understanding when issues and dilemmas arise. Respect, trust, and the preservation of individual integrity are also important aspects of collaboration.
>
> I have a true and heart-felt feeling of collaboration with the teachers in the learning community. We have a common, explicit purpose, we talk often about beliefs, values, and understandings. In fact, they drive everything we do. We respect and trust one another,

we value individual perspectives and feel comfortable disagreeing and arguing.

However, the staff as a whole . . . does not collaborate. We may consult, bargain, negotiate but we are not collaborative. . . . don't share a common purpose, have respectful and trusting relationships, don't spend much time talking about beliefs and values.

. . . makes me think about John's comments at the staff meeting about the voting last year and the sense of . . . "winners" and "losers." I empathized with John, as our team was feeling the same alienation and lack of support. It seems that small decisions and changes are slowly undermining our team's work.

On every matter that was significant to their story, Sara's team were out voted. The view of voting as voice and democracy did not fit with what she knew to be collaborative. Clearly there were two very different and conflicting stories being lived and Sara recognized it. She knew that her practice was shaped by the conflict and that, as a result, she was not doing her best work with her students. She felt unsupported and frustrated. She felt that she had little control over things and she recognized how the dominant story was shaping her practice. She also knew that her principal supported the dominant story and she worried about her learning community and what would happen to their alternative story.

CHAPTER 6

Changing a Story of School

Annie Davies

Imagine an elegant glassed-in foyer to an elementary school—a foyer rising two stories, with an open staircase to the left and a vaulted glass roof. Imagine this space hung with 20 or so multicolored banners, designed by children for a city celebration. Imagine the children's parents sewing the banners, according to exact size specifications, in beautiful translucent materials—each parent sewing two banners—one to remain in the school and a second for display at various public locations. Imagine the uniqueness of each banner, the symbols of the event depicted in the children's art. Imagine the banners hung with care, in a three-tiered effect, on fine wires stretching wall to wall across the school foyer.

Entering this school as a researcher was to enter a sea of color. Climbing the stairs—climbing up through the banners—gave me a sense of being enveloped in children's art. As a visitor to the school I was immediately aware of an environment honoring children's work. There was a special feeling about this building. It was vibrant, alive, its hallways filled with quality displays. Then one day, just weeks into a new school year, the banners disappeared from the foyer. I was puzzled. Had they been taken down to be cleaned? That was a possibility. At recess that day, amid the buzz of staff room chatter, I asked a couple of the teachers in my research study about the disappearance of the banners.

Jeff said, "I think they're being cleaned and then they'll go back up again."

But Ellen explained, "No, I don't think so. The caretaker told me that the principal doesn't like clutter. He asked him to take them down. They're not going back up."

I was surprised that Jeff and Ellen's stories differed. I asked them if their new principal, Paul, had consulted the staff about the banners.

Ellen answered, "No, there's been no discussion at all at our staff meetings, but some other banners from the library have also been taken down. They'd been hanging there for about 12 years. Children made them when the school was first opened."

"It's like history being taken down—history being whited out. I can't believe it," Jeff reflected.

"But Paul asked the librarian if she was married to those banners and she said, 'No,' because she hadn't been in the school when they were made by the children. Those banners were made of felt. They were probably dusty—but you wouldn't know that, just looking at them," said Ellen.

Turning to me, Jeff continued, "Well this new principal of ours is sure being teased a lot about being a neat freak. Perhaps taking down the banners is all about having a tidy school. You know it fits with Paul's improvements in the office—the new cupboard units and teacher mailboxes to match the gray-and-burgundy color scheme of the secretarial stations. And look at this staff room—we've got a white board, new chairs, and these small round tables that allow us to sit in clusters. Paul's also mentioned new blinds for the windows instead of the dusty curtains."

"Jeff, I think you're right," Ellen mused. "I think Paul's on a cleanup mission. I was so surprised the other afternoon when he announced the visit of the superintendent. He asked the children over the P.A. to make sure their jackets and shoes were tidy, at the coat hooks in the hallways, because of the special visitor."

"So how the school looks is important to Paul and it's important to all of us too but what I'm seeing is Paul's unilateral decision making when it comes to the entrance hall, the office, the staff room, and hallways. These spaces are quite different from our classrooms, aren't they? I can see why he asked the librarian if the felt banners could come down. They were in her space. The entrance hall is nobody's space. That's probably why Paul didn't think to ask us," Jeff suggested.

"But Jeff, these are important spaces. They speak volumes about this school. Shouldn't we have been consulted?" Ellen wondered. "The problem now is that we're silenced. Nobody can say, 'Paul, how come you did that?' All we can do is have these kinds of conversations that feel like we're gossiping."

"It doesn't seem to make sense, does it?" said Jeff with a sigh. "These spaces connect us. They link us together as a school. Perhaps I feel this way because I was on staff, 7 years ago, when the banners in the foyer were made. To me they're a symbol of what this school is all about. The banners symbolize our commitment to children. Maybe this is a wake-up call? Maybe we're about something different now? But what is it?"

Jeff's questions stayed with me long after he and Ellen returned to their classes. Their conversation helped me to see how quickly the landscape was changing with Paul's arrival. Paul had very definite ideas about the out-of-classroom place—ideas he enacted swiftly. He took pride in the image he was creating for the school. He delighted in each change and made sure that visitors, such as myself, were aware of his shaping influence. But Jeff was troubled. He was suddenly aware that the story of school, as he had known it, was changing.

I sought Jeff out a few days later and asked him to tell me more about how he saw the banners as symbols on the landscape. Sitting at his desk, he began. "To me those banners are a celebration of children's work. They take me back to conversations years ago when, as a staff, we spoke about validating children's work. We saw our classrooms as workshops and the hallways were the places where work would be displayed for a larger audience. Our administrators then spent a number of weekends putting up additional bulletin boards on every available wall. The children's work was always a talking point because of its visibility. That was the idea—that anyone in the school would be immediately captivated by the creativity and quality of the work on view. Visitors to the school were effusive in their praise. The banners symbolized, for me, the collective conscience of all those teachers who have shaped the fine reputation of this school. The banners also symbolized children and parents working together to produce works of art, meant to be treasured. So what does it mean when those banners are removed?"

For Jeff, the removal of the banners was felt as a loss whereas Paul's story appeared to be that of giving the school a new look. Paul was doubtless unaware of the conflicting stories being told and retold, both within the school and outside the building. Paul had a vision and a very definite sense of direction, but it appeared that the teachers and perhaps the parents too were unaware of the new story of school that Paul was intent on creating.

In the absence of a shared vision, teachers such as Jeff and Ellen can be seen attempting to make sense of their experience in private conversation. Jeff's response prompts Ellen to think harder about her initial acceptance of the principal's decision. At first, Paul's authority is unquestioned by Ellen. If the principal views the banners as clutter, then that is reason enough for him to ask the caretaker to remove them. Whereas Paul negotiates the removal of the additional banners in the library, with the librarian, Ellen concedes that dust is a likely factor. In this way Ellen arrives at a story allowing her to make sense of her principal's actions. But as Ellen continues to talk to Jeff she revises her viewpoint. She wonders, "Shouldn't we have been consulted?" Ellen's question is an important one. It is connected to the new story of school being authored by Paul. It is connected to the story of principal he is living out and to Paul's narrative. If the staff had been consulted it would be possible to tell this story as one in which the new principal modeled a collaborative decision-making process. It is Jeff who names Paul's actions as "unilateral decision making" concerning particular spaces on the out-of-classroom place. But Jeff sees his principal dealing quite differently with teaching spaces that are clearly the terrain of particular teachers. Ellen concludes that Paul's decisions, concerning the out-of-classroom places, silence the staff. She feels a degree of guilt in gossiping about the events in a secretive manner. Perhaps her awakening to the complexity of the landscape causes her discomfort.

For both teachers and for me, the conversation is an awakening, or as Jeff puts it, "a wake-up call." The landscape is changing, but are the changes merely cosmetic? For Jeff the answer is no. Paul's desire to improve the school by taking down the banners violates Jeff's deeply held beliefs regarding the symbolic meaning the banners hold for him. In the safety of his in-classroom place, Jeff can voice his concerns and feelings of uncertainty. However, neither he nor Ellen can risk raising their concerns on the broader landscape where Paul's stories of school improvement have free rein.

My conversation with Jeff caused me to seek out Kate, the teacher librarian. I wanted to hear her story firsthand. Leaning on the card-catalog drawers, she began.

"The felt banners were suspended on a high wire stretching wall to wall across the library. They were attractive and helped to break up this huge space. In some ways they acted as a sound buffer too. When you have a space that goes up two stories, you need decoration, otherwise it can look sterile and bleak. When Paul wanted the felt banners removed, I felt I could go along with his request because of the other fabulous works of art on the walls. Those wall hangings up there have been in place since the early 1980s and every visitor to this school remarks on their uniqueness and beauty."

Like Kate, I admired the two massive wall hangings mounted on the back wall of the library. One hung from close to the ceiling to the top of the book shelves. It was a fabric quilt made of individual pictures, each designed by a child and sewn by parents as a gift to the school in its opening year. The wall hangings were made under the direction of Heidi, the art specialist at the time. The following year Heidi made a second fabric banner, different in size and theme, with children's images of fairy-tale characters sewn in vibrant colors. As Kate and I looked at the wall hangings and contemplated their historical significance, she continued her story.

"After I agreed the felt banners could be removed, Paul pointed at Heidi's wall hangings and said, 'What are those things all about?' His words had a ring of disapproval. I knew he didn't like them. I had the sense he felt the walls should be free of clutter. I overheard him telling another staff member, 'Oh, yeah, those have to go.' But I said, 'No way! Those have to stay. I like a colorful space.' Paul didn't push me to take them down, but he remarked, 'Well, the school's scheduled for repainting. They'll have to come down then.' His words gave me an uneasy feeling—puzzlement and disbelief all rolled into one. Then some days later, a former student, Mark, came by the library on his way to pick up his little brother in Grade 1. When Mark saw me, he immediately said,

'Oh Mrs. Manning you've taken down the banners! I hope you're not going to take the big ones down. Don't ever do that. The school just wouldn't be the same.' I assured Mark that I loved the wall hangings just as much as he did and I certainly would never remove them. This brief conversation brought back the same uneasy feeling I'd had in conversation with Paul. I realized I was feeling guilty—guilty because the felt banners were gone and I didn't know where. They were taken down by the caretaker at the weekend when nobody was around. I hadn't thought to suggest that at the very least, we should store them. I realized Mark had a sense of history, a sense of the meaning residing in treasured objects, and now I'm reluctant to even ask where the felt banners went."

Reflecting on Kate's story, I think about the way that she was able to speak her mind in her in-classroom place. She saw the library as her space and she was able to challenge Paul's authority. In Paul's response to her there is, however, the inevitability of the banners coming down on the arrival of the school district's painting crew. The uneasy feeling that Kate experiences deepens following her conversation with Mark. In assuring Mark that she will not take down the wall hangings, she recognizes the untenable position she is in. Kate says nothing on the out-of-classroom place—to do so would be unprofessional. In this regard Kate is like Jeff and Ellen. She is silenced. In silence she awaits the painters.

Some weeks later, on one of my research visits, Jeff said, "Can we have lunch together? I've got some interesting news to tell you. I'd feel more comfortable talking over a pizza. It's really important for me to make sense of the changes happening in the building. I feel as though I can't talk about this in school, not even to Ellen. I worry about being unprofessional."

Sipping a Coke at the restaurant, I listen to Jeff.

Last night, after my floor hockey game, I went for a beer and just happened to strike up a conversation with a player on the other team. Guess what, he was the new principal of Paul's old school. He got talking about all the renovations Paul had been responsible for at that school. He'd spruced up the office with new gray desk units that secretaries get to sit behind and the teachers can't go and monkey around with their stuff. The staffroom was new and it had loveseats. They were all nicely covered and the walls were painted and it was very neat. Now when the previous principal was there, it wasn't neat. So as he was telling me all of this I was thinking that somehow Paul's been given a cleanup story and he's come here to smarten things up— to spruce up the place a little bit. The staff at Paul's old school really like what he did and the new principal told me how much he admired him and how easy it was to just follow in his footsteps. So I think Paul's trying to live out that story with us. He's expecting the same response—that we'll like it too. What do you think?

"It's true—principals are given a story by the system when they take over a new assignment," I replied.

"Yes, and perhaps the story is we've lost our glitter. We need shaping up and Paul's here to remind us that this is a place of polish and professionalism and efficiency. Having the painters come is the perfect way to clean up an entire school. Wow, it blows my mind, particularly when I think about the last time the painters were here, just doing touch-up work, because they said, 'This school's in good shape.' Now, just 2 years later, the whole place needs a face-lift."

The Painters: The Landscape Changes

The painters did not come until fall of the following year. By this time Kate Manning had retired, keeping her promise to Mark. But the wall hangings did come down. I happened to be in the school the day the library was being painted. The wall hangings were draped over the library carrels as the painters went about their work. I asked a couple of the teachers if the wall hangings were going back up. "Oh no," they said and that seemed to be common knowledge. "They'll probably be thrown out," one teacher said, "they're pretty dusty."

Troubled by this comment, I said nothing. I wrestled with the fact that I was a visitor in the school, a researcher. I thought about the way that Paul had welcomed me that day, saying, "What do you think of the new paint job? Oh, and before you leave make sure you check out the latest staff room renovations." But I did not have the heart to visit the staff room and I could only look at the gray walls with burgundy trim and feel silent—silent on the out-of-classroom place, remembering Kate Manning's story of Mark.

Once home, I made the decision to phone Jeff. In seconds he came up with three suggestions for what to do with the wall hangings. "It makes sense to phone Heidi. She's a high school art teacher now. I know her school. I'll tell her what's happening and see if she wants the wall hangings. It's only right that she should be asked. If Heidi says no, then I bet the museum would be interested and if not, then I could approach the university. There's all sorts of children's art work hanging there."

The following day Jeff phoned to say he'd been able to contact Heidi. She wanted the wall hangings and would phone Paul to make arrangements to pick them up.

I heard no more about the wall hangings until some weeks later. Somehow the story found its way back to Kate Manning. Kate phoned to tell me she had felt the need to contact Heidi. She said, "I phoned her because I wanted her to know the wall hangings were admired and appreciated throughout my term as librarian. Heidi told me how surprised she was that suddenly the children's work was not valued in the way it should be. We wondered together what sense the children and parents would make of this. I told her the new librarian wanted to sweep clean—wanted to have a new look."

I was surprised that Kate had contacted Heidi—surprised because Kate had not been on staff with Heidi and yet felt compelled to contact a teacher she had never met. I was even more surprised when Kate mentioned a recent dream she had had about the library—a particularly vivid dream that she remembered clearly. She explained, "I dreamed that Paul and the new librarian put up this great modern art thing with glitzy shapes to give the appearance of a high-tech library. Right now, of course, the walls are bare. The library has no character, no personality, yet and I wonder how it will be decorated and what others will see in the decorations."

What sense do I make of Kate Manning's dream? It is a dream of a changing landscape—a dream reflecting the loss of what was—a dream reflecting teacher uncertainty. Perhaps Kate's dream is similar to Jeff's "wake-up call" and his sense that "maybe we're about something different now." And that "something different" is tied to Paul's story of school—tied to a story given to him.

In the same way that Kate's subconscious was tugging at her, I found myself constantly being tripped up by the story of the changing landscape whenever I entered the school. My own research behaved quite nicely. My field notes sat in my backpack until I had time for them. Completed chapters of my dissertation lay quietly in the black folder on my desk at home. The ethical guidelines of my work gave me a sense of security, and yet here was this other story constantly assailing me—tugging at me in the same way that Grade 1 youngsters pull on their teacher's sleeve or tap persistently on her arm to gain attention.

I found myself pulled into this story, pulled into conversations in a way I had not expected. I wanted to hear multiple accounts from those experiencing the changes on the out-of-classroom place. I began to see that there could be many perspectives, depending on how one was positioned on the landscape and on one's understanding of the landscape over time. As I thought about this, I had an urge to hear Heidi's story. I looked in the phone book and found her distinctive European name. I called on the weekend, hopeful of time to talk.

After explaining myself to Heidi, I found her eager to tell her story. She said, "When I phoned the principal, he told me the new librarian didn't want the wall hangings. She wanted to decorate the space in her own way. I can accept that, but I feel sad for the kids. The wall hangings were something they had made that gave their school some character, some personality, and now what they contributed isn't there anymore. Decorations provided an identity for a school, and now that identity has been stripped away—aesthetics disregarded. It seems to me there's a lack of respect for the school's history."

As we spoke further, Heidi made an interesting observation: "The library belongs to everyone, and I wonder about the fate of the wall hangings, if everyone had been asked. Who makes decisions in a school? It's not the children, the teachers, or the parents despite the empty promises we pay lip service to. Every new principal seems to have this need to leave a mark—a new look. In any event, I'll keep the wall hangings. I'll give them a good cleaning in the summer when I can spread them out on my lawn and perhaps in a few years the next principal will find a place for them. We can only hope."

"That's right," I said and thanked Heidi for her time. Putting the phone down, I thought about her words. They seemed to echo Jeff's sentiments about history being whited out. For Heidi the wall hangings were like a legacy from the children, one she was part of. Her comment, "Decorations provide an identity for a school," made me wonder even more about Kate Manning's dream, about new appearances, new looks. What would the landscape be like? Would the children be involved in creating a new identity? Who would be consulted?

More Paint: More Teachers' Stories on the Landscape

With the arrival of the painters, one of the teachers posed a question: "What about the logos painted on the gym walls? They can't possibly paint over those."

Paul's initial response was, "Well that has to happen because that's the way the painters' contract reads. They estimate the job on an hourly rate and away they go. They're not going to paint around all of those logos. The cost could be astronomical." Paul's response did not satisfy the staff, because the gym, unlike the library, belonged to a great many of the teachers who taught their own daily physical education lessons. They had a vested interest in the appearance of the gym; they liked the decor, and there was a story attached to the painted logos.

These had been painted to commemorate the same city celebration as marked by the banners that had hung in the foyer. From that standpoint they were historical. Jeff was able to provide me with the story:

"It was Todd, one of the physical education specialists, who suggested painting the official city celebration logo on the back wall of the gym. The principal at that time thought it was a great idea and Todd was delighted because he'd wanted to do something like that for some time. He thought our high school–size gym was such a bleak space—like a big white barn, two stories high. Todd was a calligrapher, so the principal had no worries about the quality of his work. He was also a prominent track and field official and had been involved in the Commonwealth Games. Todd was keen to decorate the gym with some sports logos. Once he got started, the results were so terrific that he just kept going. The principal even helped, and together they completed well over 20 logos. It was hours of work, as you can guess. The end result was magnificent and everyone really saw Todd's work as a gift to the school. He'd have a fit if he knew the painters were here. He's on a sabbatical right now, but he'll be back in September."

The topic of the painters and the gym was keenly discussed by the teachers on the out-of-classroom place. The suggestion was made that the gym looked fine—it did not need painting. It was clear that no one wanted to lose the logos. At a staff meeting, Roberta, a teacher highly regarded by her colleagues and by the school administrators, too, made the suggestion that a volunteer parent group could paint around the logos and prepare them for the less time-consuming roller work of the painters. "And what was the outcome of all of this" I asked Jeff.

"Well, it was really important that Roberta spoke up as she did because she's seen as a master teacher, a hard worker, a person who doesn't complain and who is always supportive of her administration. On top of all that, she's got a great sense of humor, so when Paul suggested that she could organize the volunteers, she quipped back, 'Are you kidding? I'm a classroom teacher.' Everyone laughed, and Paul said, 'Well the admin team will take a look at this.' Now if I'd made that suggestion, I think the idea would have been dismissed and someone would have said, 'Oh, dream on, Jeff.' But when Roberta spoke, it really made the administrators think again. And the end result of all of this was a compromise. The painters did the work but only half of the logos were saved. Todd heard about what was happening. He came in and talked to Paul. He told him how disappointed he was. And I guess I share Todd's disappointment too. When I come to school now, it's like it could be any school. It's just a school. It's bricks and it's stairwells and it's corridors. Is that how a school should feel?"

For Jeff the loss of the banners and logos translates to a loss of identity. His school, freshly painted as it is, feels "like it could be any school." In my view, Jeff experiences a loss of his sense of place. His words trouble me. I find myself retelling his story at my research-group meeting, where a member of the group raises more questions. "Do we know who it is we are and what story we are constructing for ourselves if we have no place? What does place have to do with our stories? And what about the children who come to our classrooms? Do they want to have a sense of place? We tell ourselves they do."

CHAPTER 7

An ESL Instructor's Teaching Stories in a Shifting Landscape

Ming Fang He, JoAnn Phillion, and Norman Beach

"It would be great to have a volunteer to monitor my class. I want the volunteer to make sure that my students don't revert to their first languages. Sometimes my students want the information so much that they don't go through the process that is the most important for them: Figure out the information by asking questions in English. They would just translate."

"How about if we come to your classroom and do volunteer work and research at the same time?"

"That sounds great! I'll certainly enjoy it." (Conversation between Norman, Ming Fang, and JoAnn, July 1995)

We had been working in an adult English as a second language (ESL) site of the City Board of Education for 2 years. In the 2nd year of the research we came to know Norman. As we worked as volunteers and researchers in his class, we began to understand his story of teaching. We also shared our stories of adult ESL teaching with him.

Since 1986, Norman has been teaching for the Adult ESL Center of the City Board of Education. This center is situated in a large metropolitan city. It is within an inner-city secondary school and belongs to the Continuing Education Department of the City Board. The center has many program branches, among them French as a second language, archaeological resources, general interest and credit courses, parenting, adult ESL, adult basic education, multicultural workplace, senior courses and summer courses. Under the supervision of the superintendent of the City Board, the adult ESL program aims to provide new immigrants with language skills, life skills, and orientation to Canadian law, government, and society; and to facilitate new immigrants' full participation in all aspects of a multicultural society.

Norman was one of the 150 adult ESL instructors in this center. These instructors worked with ten lead instructors, an administrator, library resource facilitator, reception assessment referral facilitator, multicultural workplace facilitator, staff development facilitator, materials development facilitator, secretary, clerk, and receptionist. These people facilitated the management of over 400 adult ESL classes located in 80 community centers, 19 elementary and secondary school sites, and other locations.

The class we were involved with was situated in a public school at the west end of the city. It was an intermediate class. Most of the students were female, from their mid-20s to mid-60s. The students were from Chile, Turkey, Iraq, mainland China, Hong Kong, Taiwan, Burma, and Vietnam. Some were newcomers to Canada. Some worked part time, some had been laid off. There were 20 students registered in Norman's class, the usual attendance being around 15. Students would come and go according to their needs and life goals. Norman had another class in a community center a 10-minute walk from the school, with a half-hour interval between his public school class and that in the community center. Norman also worked as an ESL instructor in a night class in a public school in the east end of the city.

In the following section, we will retell Norman's story of teaching by beginning with one of his classes. This was scheduled to begin at 9:00 a.m. When we arrived, Norman's students were waiting in the school hallway, some chatting with Norman, others looking at posters made by the elementary students in different styles reflective of their diverse backgrounds. Ping, the oldest student in the class, was reading an English newspaper and mouthing the words. Aisha was telling people about her citizenship interview. Maria rushed in from her morning shift in a restaurant. Norman's classroom was being used for the school psychological counseling workshop. He had just been informed by the principal that his class had to be postponed for 20 minutes. At 9:20 a.m., when we got into the classroom, Norman apologized to his students. He explained why they were delayed while he drew a selection ward map on the blackboard. He tried to mark out the borders between each ward area, but could not find any colored chalk. Chang went to a cabinet and gave Norman several pieces that she had hidden for him. Chang did organizational work for the class, such as making tea and coffee and scheduling who was to bring food. Norman asked the students to tell us what had happened yesterday, encouraging them to review what they had covered in the previous class. He had new and regular students introduce each other:

Norman: Yin, could you introduce the lady on your left to the gentleman on your right?

Yin: OK. But I don't know his name yet.
Norman: Ask him (smiling).
Yin: How to pronounce your last name.
Huang: Huang.
Yin: This is Chen Huang. This is Ming Fang.
Ming Fang: Ming Fang He.
Yin: OK, this is Ming Fang He. She is a volunteer in our class. He helped Norman teach us.
Norman: I know when you speak Chinese, there's no difference between "she" and "he." Actually, to avoid the confusion between "she" and "he," you can use "this is." When you speak English, you need to remember the difference between "she" and "he."
Yin: (Smiles).
Chai: We have few people attended the class.
Norman: Yesterday is past. So we?
Students: We had.
Chai: Oh, we only had eight. Norman was nervous. We are, oh, we were nervous.
Norman: Why was I nervous?
Students: Because your supervisor visit our class.
Norman: Right, but "visited," I told my supervisor that was very unusual.
Students: Yeah, we usually have a lot of people.

Students regretted having missed the class. Ha said she had a doctor's appointment. Vesna said her son was sick. Mohammed said his boss called him back to work. Aisha said she had to attend a citizenship interview. Norman told the students not to worry about it. However, Norman told us that he was frustrated by the fact that he had to pay more attention to the numbers of the students than concentrating on curriculum planning, resource exploration, and listening to students' talk. "Because of budget cuts, there is more emphasis on the numbers in the class. This affects my morale. I think it drains the personal and professional relationship," Norman said. He added that he would call his students the night before the lead instructor visited his class to ensure that they showed up. He felt pushy but he did it anyway.

Norman: Congratulations, Aisha, you are a Canadian citizen now.
Students: Yah, congratulations.
Norman: Don't worry about it. I understand sometimes you have something important to do. So you can't come to class. The reason I let you talk about it is to let you practice your English. I don't know what my lead is going to do. But anyhow she won't judge our class by a one-time visit. Our class is usually crowded, right?

The students kept regretting their absence. We heard some of them blaming each other. Norman finished drawing the map. He wrote down the students' names and asked them to figure out in which ward they lived. Norman encouraged his learners to become involved in the voting process. Ming Fang, who was also a part-time ESL instructor, told Norman that she did the same thing in her class. She felt it was important for learners to become interested in what was happening in Canadian society. Norman wrote the abbreviations of the major political parties on the blackboard and asked the students for the full names. He began to explain the meaning of the abbreviations and the philosophy of each political party.

At 9:45 a.m. we split into groups. Norman did an activity to help students ask and answer questions about the political parties. He wrote sentence patterns on the blackboard. He integrated structure, function, grammar, and pronunciation into the voting process. Ping tried to answer every question Norman asked. Norman invited other students to enter the discussion. In a previous conversation, he had told us:

> I think that my students have to negotiate their own way through their uncertainties and confusion, since in their workplace they can't have a teacher beside them to clear up those misunderstandings. I usually organize my class according to the theme, while other language elements are sort of an ad hoc thing. I rely on circulating as much as possible in individual, pair, and group work, looking at the students' writing, and listening to their role-plays and discussions. If there are any new grammatical structures or vocabulary my students can't utilize in their practice, I would switch the lesson focus and reteach those elements. For instance, when a large number of students are looking for jobs, we would do a class on job applications and interview processes in order to get my students ready for the job market. (Interview, September 1995)

One woman in JoAnn's group came up with an interesting metaphor: The platform of the various parties was like a shell, and it was rather empty. In that way people who were voting could put almost any ideas they had into the shell. Some learners wondered what the politicians would be like after they got elected. Some learners had no interest in politics. What they really cared about was survival in Canadian society. Four of Ming Fang's group members were Chinese, and they tried to lure her into speaking their language. Norman smiled and said he would appreciate it if Ming Fang could help them to speak as much English as possible.

Ping told stories about coming to Canada 40 years ago. The first time he took a Canadian train, he could not speak one word of English. He was starving but did not know how to say "sandwiches" or "milk." He could only point to the food he wanted. Some people politely smiled at him, others frowned. Ping had come to Norman's class 6 years ago, after he had retired and settled in the city. Since then he had attended classes off and on, although he did not need English in order to make a living. His knowledge of English grammar was very limited, yet he was one of the students in the class who knew most about Canadian culture. In class he often shared stories of his culture- and language-shock experiences. As long as he was able to communicate, he paid little attention to the rules of grammar, no matter how hard Norman tried to influence him to develop native speaking skills. Norman told us: "Ping's spoken English hasn't greatly improved, although he has made a lot of progress in his listening comprehension. I tried several times to suggest to Ping that he move to a higher-level conversation class. But Ping kept coming back to my class. I don't know why."

At 10:15 there was a break. Some students had brought food and drinks. Chang made tea and coffee and served green-onion pancakes that she had brought from the breakfast program in which she worked at another school. She told us that she got up very early to make breakfast for the children in the school while her own children were still sleeping at home, this being the only job she could get. Weijuan, Theresa, and Mai shared the food they brought while telling stories of their daily lives. Some students offered Norman cookies and asked him questions; others discussed their plans to open small businesses. Norman suggested that they go to an ESL workshop on how to start a small business. He promised to have several classes on that topic.

At 10:30, the class continued. Norman mentioned his summer leave, and the probability of a supply teacher arriving for the summer. However, because of budget cuts, school board trustees might close the class. If students really wanted the summer class, they had to either write a letter or talk to the trustees to voice their opinion. Norman wrote the trustees' names and telephone numbers on the board. He asked his students to discuss where to send the letters and how to speak to the trustees. Norman told them: "Don't worry about your English. Anyhow, the trustees know that you are still learning English. Just get the message across; that is most important. If you feel more comfortable speaking your own languages when you phone the trustees, you can ask for one who speaks that language." The students decided to write letters. At 11:00 a.m., some students began to leave to go to work or join their children in their lunch breaks. The class finished at 11:20. We gave Norman a lift to the community center; he had to rush to make his 11:30 class. In the car we shared our thoughts and feelings about that day's class. We promised that we would show him the field notes that we were going to write about his class.

In a cafeteria one day, Norman read the field notes. He told us that the way in which he taught his class had a lot to do with how he saw himself as an ESL instructor, which was not only as an instructor, but also as a liaison between English Canadian society and the students. Since he was often the first English Canadian whom students got to know, he felt like a "welcoming ambassador" for Canada. He also perceived himself as a social facilitator helping people feel comfortable enough to communicate. He shared personal stories with students in order to create an environment where students could express themselves freely. He facilitated students' development of life skills, language skills, and political awareness. Through interaction with his students, he helped them prepare to exercise their rights and responsibilities as Canadian citizens in the community. He and his students changed the classroom from a collection of strangers into a community of friends.

Norman continues to help his students not only inside the classroom, but outside as well, with settlement issues, immigration, parenting, family and marital problems, and appropriate agencies. Sometimes he does research for his students. For instance, one of his students had a hearing problem. He telephoned the Canadian Hearing Society to obtain information about available equipment. Norman realizes that helping students becomes an ESL instructor's obligation, although he or she is only paid for instructional hours. He said:

> In a way that is one of the reasons that we are in the job. We want to connect with people and help them out. We wouldn't want to see that disappear from the job. It should be recognized that we do work outside of class. Our lesson-planning time is never paid. But we wouldn't want to ever reach the point where we thought that everything had a monetary value. (Journal entry, August 1995)

Through our connection with Norman, we began to understand that his way of teaching was connected to the way that he was educated and the experiences he had. He obtained a bachelor of arts degree in history from Carleton University. He had an interest in music, arts, and literature and intended to become a writer. After he worked for a publishing company for a short time, he attended teachers college. He was fascinated by the idea of progressive education and went to Central America, where he worked as an English teacher. When he returned to Canada, he developed ideas and teaching methodologies based on his ESL certificate courses at a university and on his teaching experiences. He taught ESL to children in Northern Quebec, where he experienced difficulties adjusting to his new environment. Later he traveled in mainland China, India, Morocco, and South America.

The place where Norman lives, the place where he teaches, and the place where his students learn and live are inseparable. Most ESL instructors only work on a part-time basis. In order to survive, they have to have second or third jobs. They are paid by the hour and lesson-planning time is not paid. Most of them have had exposure to a second culture and language. Their knowledge base has to touch upon a variety of resources, such as Canadian culture, history, and government, in order to facilitate their students' full participation in Canadian society. Every day they rush to and from their different employment sites. Their classes could be closed any day if the student number is low. They actively help students to comprehend the language and to develop cultural awareness in a new society. They are rewarded to see students find a job and survive happily in Canada. Meanwhile, their students' coming and going changes the dynamics of the classroom. Physically, their classrooms are located in any available space, squeezed into formal institutions, community agencies, libraries, and apartment buildings. The movable classrooms where they create their stories of teaching, the students' coming and going, and the unstable occupations they are in shape their personal and professional lives in a shifting landscape.

Norman told us that he has had to move into a small room in a community center, since the school needed the classroom he was using. The principal did the best she could, but her first priority would always be the school's needs. "We are considered to be a group of people coming from outside. We are always going to be a lower priority." Norman also related that nowadays his morale was very low. His mental energy had started to flag due to the cumulative effect of the bad news around budget cuts. He found it disheartening that desperation had crept into the daily conversation in his workplace, and was worried that the situation would hurt personal and professional relationships. Norman has been actively involved in voluntarily working with his union as newsletter editor. He interviewed parents, children, teachers and principals to voice their needs and concerns about immigrant education and its relationship to public school education. Norman is thinking of finding a job in the Separate School Board and considering the possibility of working in a credit program that has more stability than the adult ESL programs, or going abroad to teach foreign students. Norman does not want to change his profession.

PART II

Reflections on Knowledge, Context, and Identity

In Chapter 1, and in the Introduction to Part I, we name and describe the main terms and ideas at work in our attempt to understand storied identity and storied landscapes. Part I contains a set of stories in which these terms and ideas help make sense of teacher practice. In Part II we reflect upon the stories and the terms and ideas to help us make links among teacher knowledge, teaching context, and teacher identity. In Part II we make no attempt to give equal time and space to the chapters of Part I. We weave the stories of Part I in and out of the chapters of Part II.

CHAPTER 8

Curriculum Making
and Teacher Identity

In the preceding chapters we read stories of teachers and teachers' stories. At a first-level reading the stories are of curriculum making. At this level they are accounts of curriculum making, with its various deliberations and considerations: They relate to teacher preference, to student interests and activities, to conduit-delivered policies and guidelines, to activities and people outside the classroom, and to teacher biographies.

In Huber's story we see her as a teacher who is a responsive curriculum maker. In this reading she is initially responsive in her curriculum making to the outside world as delivered through the conduit. As things progress, however, she becomes responsive to the situation in which she finds herself, and particularly to the children's lives. In Whelan's story we see her making curriculum with children and their parents in parent-teacher-student conferences. For Whelan, these conferences are relational events and are part of her curriculum making. They are curricular because she expects the children to articulate and give back the content and meaning of their education to their teacher and to their parents. In Quan, Phillion, and He's story of Nancy we see Nancy making curriculum in a large-group lecture format. She delivers the conduit-prescribed nursing curriculum and examines the students' ability to complete the curriculum.

Seen in the terms of the professional knowledge landscape, these three sets of stories represent, and reveal, different ways in which teachers' curriculum making within the classroom is connected to the out-of-classroom places and to different responses to what comes down the respective conduits.

Huber initially plans a curriculum paying careful attention to the various curriculum guides delivered to her by the conduit. She artfully weaves a planned curriculum using a metaphor of a garden, and structures her time and space in the classroom to fulfill curricular requirements. Things, however, are complicated when she meets the children and finds herself making curriculum in response to their lives. In Whelan's case we see her creating a curriculum plan for student conferences, a plan responsive to children and their parents. This plan, however, is brought into question by other teachers and by the conduit in a sequence of school settings in which she finds herself. In the story of Nancy we see a nursing educator who finds a way to make curriculum with her nursing students that fits her knowledge and conduit-prescribed mandates despite difficult working conditions.

This quick curricular reading of these three chapters provides a useful, albeit somewhat technical, understanding of these teachers' lives as curriculum makers. Much depends on the teachers' personal practical knowledge and the curricular situations in which they find themselves. The set of landscape terms used above is helpful in sorting out what is happening in the complex world of curriculum making. We name teachers' curricular experience when we speak of conduits, of out-of-classroom places, of people in relationship, of students.

But understanding the making of curriculum in landscape terms is only the tip of the iceberg. A great deal more is happening, as our next level reading of the three sets of stories will show.

The first reading skips over the dilemmas that, in the end, make the difference to both the participants and their curriculum. In Huber's story what is not seen in the surface reading of her planning intentions, and the curricular adaptations she makes as she meets her children, is the sense of the dilemmas she faces. Her sense of dilemma is conveyed by her use of words such as *stunned* and the description of the hours she spends in conversations with Shaun, her junior teaching partner. In Whelan's story what is not seen in the first reading of her evolution of responses to her changing situation vis-à-vis student conferences is the intensity of the dilemma she felt around those conferences. The passion with which she tries to maintain her notion of conferences as part of curriculum making is expressed in phrases such as *buckling under* and, conversely, *honoring what I have come to know*. In the story of Nancy what is not seen in the first reading of her use of conduit-prescribed curriculum making is the intensity of the dilemma she experiences as seen indirectly and biographically as she moves in and out of nursing and psychology.

In sum, there is a great deal of intensity about the curriculum-making process that is not entirely explained by the first curricular reading. For us, the intensity of the dilemmas is a sign of something important to understanding education. Coming back to our iceberg metaphor, the question is, How much more lies hidden beneath the surface of these individuals' lives on the professional knowledge landscape?

The Link Between Curriculum and Teacher Identity

From several points of view, that of the casual observer or reader; that of an expert in the knowledge and skills of the practice of teaching; or that of a teaching methodologist concerned with the tactics, strategies, and methodologies of teaching, the mere existence of the dilemmas faced by the three practitioners in these stories, let alone the intensity with which those dilemmas are experienced, is puzzling. People are hired for jobs that are defined by society and spelled out in detail professionally. These are well-known conditions of employment. Furthermore, employees are taught a knowledge and skill base for their professional practice as well as proper and socially accepted ways of relating to administrative and professional requirements and to plans, teachers, students, and patients. Broadly speaking this is all made quite clear as people pass through their professional education though, of course, details are always in question. Yet, in the three stories, one teacher, Huber, appears to be so distressed at the discrepancy between what she thinks a curriculum should be and what she had planned for it as an application of policy that she feels it necessary to keep secret from others that part of her curriculum closest to her heart. Another teacher, Whelan, is concerned about the practices adopted by her colleagues and the school system over what might appear a relatively minor matter, student-teacher-parent conferences. A nursing educator, Nancy, struggles with similar discrepancies over the span of her career between what she believes she is required to do and believes she should do. She moves in and out of her profession, joining, leaving, and rejoining as she follows her urges to practice and her despair at professional incompatibilities encountered.

These stories are not unique. Indeed, in one way or another we believe that these stories all touch, in one way or another, on a grand story of the professions, at least the professions of teaching and nursing. These are relational professions. But relationship is, too, an abstraction that can be taught and, indeed, is taught in teaching and nursing. What, then, does explain the puzzling quality of these three stories, this puzzle of teaching? Let us look more closely and read, yet again, these three sets of stories.

We believe that the dilemmas experienced by the participants in these chapters, and the intensity with which they are experienced, is partly connected with the identities each teacher lives out in her work and, partially, these matters are connected to the discrepancies each experiences between her identity and the formal curricular expectations of her role. We shall unpack aspects of each participant's identity and the discrepancies experienced in what follows.

As we pursue this unpacking, it is important that we, and our readers, keep in mind our relationship to the stories discussed. Ours is a metalevel text. It is a reflective one that uses, as a basis, the three research texts written by Huber, Whelan, Quan, Phillion, and He. We did not return to the original field texts in order to provide a different perspective from that of the authors. Instead, we began with the authors' statements. Each author has, in turn, her own relationship to her participants. Huber and Whelan's work is autobiographical, Huber writing about an entire year's teaching experience and Whelan writing about her 7 years of teaching experience. Each draws heavily on field records as well as on their memories as researcher-participants. Quan, Phillion, and He's chapter on Nancy is based on one class observation combined with several conversational-style interviews in which Nancy offers statements of rules, principles, and personal philosophy having to do with her career prior to teaching. From this it is clear that the status of the chapter-stories as representative of each participant is dramatically different from case to case. In writing the metalevel text we have not, could not even if we wished, reevaluated the research texts written by each of the authors. Notwithstanding the considerable differences in the status of each story as described above, we worked with the research texts, the stories expressed in the chapters, as givens.

Huber's Story

Huber's place on the landscape is one of classroom community. She and Shaun work hard to create a space that will "feel warm and inviting" for the children. Prior to the arrival of the children, Huber's idea of a classroom community leads her and Shaun to create a special physical classroom environment. When the children arrive, the two teachers use a metaphor of the classroom as a garden to help them think through the place of individual children in the developing classroom community. Everything written in this section of Huber's chapter is testimony to the creation of classroom community and of the place of children in it: The story about the pebble serves as a metaphor for children to write about the "ripples" they create in the classroom community; *The Salamander Room* is used to demonstrate a collaborative environment; a "support circle" is used to create communal response to individual writing; *The Rag Coat* is used to make the point metaphorically that bits and pieces of an individual's experience come together to create whole cloth; and the two teachers see the contributions of each child as an analogy to a puzzle in which pieces fit together to form a circle. Children's work is displayed and their words are used to create a language of the classroom: a language of "caring," of "helping," of "encouraging."

In Huber's story, classroom community and construction of curriculum appear, at first, to be seamless. Curriculum planning to fulfill board and school mandates is naturally accomplished in a classroom community. So seamless is curriculum and community that curriculum making is barely noticeable in the story until Huber describes how the principal invited her to a dinner party given for a team of researchers and teachers scheduled for a visit to the school. At one point in the evening the principal asked Huber to explain how she was integrating curriculum around her garden metaphor and how these, in turn, were useful approaches to dealing with the school's diverse student population. It is clear from the principal's request that she saw Huber's class-room as exemplifying excellence in terms of curriculum policy. The principal saw Huber's story of teaching as supporting the story of school the principal promoted. The story of this school is one in which curriculum guidelines are met at the same time that the diverse student needs within the school are met. The principal's school story of Huber is of a teacher who is able to do that.

Huber's overall story, of course, is one of showing the seams where none appear to exist. Her opening story with Ameel and Monica is clearly designed to let the reader in on the secret that the classroom community is not all it is supposed to be. Ameel and Monica's dispute, how it is resolved, and what it represents about what is going on in the classroom, tells us nothing directly about curriculum. One might easily imagine Huber to have settled the dispute, and others as they arose, as teachers do every day, and to have proceeded quite comfortably with the day. After all, the in-classroom place, as she describes it, was quite communally oriented with the children enriching it through their activities and with the support circle resulting in thoughtful conversations. So why does Huber make the Ameel-Monica dispute the centerpiece, and why is there so much tension as the overall story unfolds? The answer is that Huber's teaching identity is strongly tied up with community. The Ameel-Monica story is evidence, for her, that her classroom community is fragile, even fraudulent. As she describes her classroom in response to the principal's request at the din-ner party, she hints that there was a great deal not said about her "discontinuities and wonders."

In the next section of her chapter, "Going Underground," the seams are sewn in bold stitches, and we get a sense of just how far she will go in her in-classroom curriculum making to maintain her teaching identity as a story of classroom community. She gives evidence for her sense that community is not working as she would like it to. She refers to "children being left out"; to "hurting words"; and to "the persistent use of anger and aggression to solve problems." The afternoons in the classroom were filled with children telling angry stories about their time on the playground. Her metaphor of "going underground" signals her break with curriculum as she searches for increasingly deeper ways of creating community. After much deliberation on what to do, she and Shaun held a session with students to talk about these concerns.

In the last section of the chapter, "Listening to and Responding," Huber describes the unfolding of the afternoon plan. She begins a second support circle in the afternoon, one in which children tell personal stories. Afternoon curriculum making becomes what she refers to as "mutually negotiated construction" with the children. The section unfolds as she tells a series of stories, each one of which can be read as a story that confirms a growing sense of classroom community. In the Tyler story, for example, the children encircle Tyler and wish him well as he leaves. This occurs, notwithstanding the fact that Tyler is viewed as somewhat of a class outcast. In Ameel's story of his grandfather's death, the community is illustrated as children create a safe place for Ameel to tell his story, as support is given back to him, and as other students tell stories in response to his. The chapter concludes by Huber's writing that the classroom, while moving deeper underground, was "uncovering important self-truths which were shaping the surface of our classroom landscape."

Although it is clear from this that Huber's identity is closely tied to classroom community, to the extent that she is prepared to abandon parts of the planned curriculum, she does so only after a great deal of soul searching. This is not an easy transition for her. In "Going Underground," the split between the planned curriculum and community becomes a clear identity issue for her. She knows that one of the stories for her to live by is to continue with the curriculum plan and to live out the principal's story of school. She also knows that the story of community is more compelling for her. Her dilemma is that she cannot live out both stories as she had originally imagined at the beginning of the year. Now she begins to "dread the afternoon" because she spends so much time listening to children's stories instead of following her "teacher plan" to cover a variety of shared reading activities. She worries that they rarely get to these activities. She and Shaun spend time worrying about this after school and eventually take the action described above. It is a hard-won action—one in which she has to choose one of the two "voices conversing in my mind," each signifying a different plotline she might live by. The strongest voice, the plotline she chooses, is one of building classroom community.

As if this dilemma, intense and sometimes as debilitating as it was, was not enough, Huber found herself unable to talk about it with anyone other than Shaun, who shared her classroom space. She knew her chosen story to live by was in conflict with the principal's story of school and the school's story of her. This is what she was getting at when she described the dinner party at the principal's home and explained that she only told a cover story. What she told was a story of a successful classroom community, the story told in the section "Contextualizing Our Place on the Landscape." She is not prepared to allow others to tell a different story of her.

Whelan's Story

Whelan's identity, her story to live by, is clearly connected to the student-teacher-parent conferences, her experiences of which she traces over the better part of her 7-year teaching career. These conferences are not, for Whelan, merely an example of an aspect of curriculum as, for instance, a unit on animals or a trip to the zoo might be. For her, conferences are an integral part, a major moment, in her rhythm of curriculum making. Curriculum is temporal. It is made over time, over the days, weeks, and months of a year. Just as there are moments when lessons are begun, ideas initiated, projects undertaken, there are moments when students, teachers, and parents come together to assess progress. These moments are fundamentally curricular for Whelan because they are planned educational experiences. They are moments that are primarily led by students who, as she says, are the "key communicators as they celebrated their learning and growth."

And, while growth was being celebrated, growth took place. She referred to the conferences at her second school as "learning conferences," "rich growth experiences for everyone involved." The child learned by pulling together experiences and articulating them to others and, through that process, made new meaning of them. Teachers learned about teaching and learning by observing this process and parents learned something of what educational growth meant for their child. Thus, while it is common to think of parent-teacher interviews as occasions for conveying summative information about a child's progress, sessions that normally occur following an assessment and testing period, for Whelan, they are a curricular activity in which students, teachers, and parents are educated.

In Whelan's chapter we see her describe herself as a passionate curriculum maker: In the story she lives by she describes her classroom as full of "rich, cherished moments which were a part of every day that the children and I spent together." Her passion is for her story of curriculum as one of relationships among children and teachers as they live out a personal journey. For her, this means that samples of student work are demonstrations, and evidence, of the journey. Her story to live by, and the curriculum she makes in her classroom, including conferences, are one and the same: They, too, are seamless.

Even this way of understanding Whelan's identity as a teacher is puzzling without an understanding, too, of the metaphor of the journey that shapes her story to live by. Without an understanding of metaphor as part of embodied knowledge, a reader might imagine that these metaphors are lightly chosen and that Whelan could merely substitute a different metaphor, one in which conferences would, then, no longer be as important. Given our view of metaphors as part of a teacher's embodied knowledge, as central to his or her story to live by, this is not a possibility for Whelan. Imagine for a moment those journeys that we see as life shaping. These are journeys that we need to tell stories of to those closest to us. So it is for Whelan's classroom journey with students. In her story to live by the children need to tell stories of their life-shaping journeys to their parents and to their teacher.

Whelan's account of her 2nd year of teaching in the section Companions on the Journey is the place in her chapter where this seamlessness is most evident. This is where she is able to live out the journey metaphor, especially as she describes the student-parent-teacher conferences. She illustrates the importance of a relational curriculum and how it is carried over into conferences in her story of Sarah. In her description of the conference with Sarah and her parents, we see her idea of curriculum as relationship in mutually shared journies and her story to live by as someone who does that in what appears to be complete harmony. She referred to the setting as being "much like a family gathered at the supper table." As she talks about this she does so in curricular terms and refers to the "rich growth experiences for everyone involved." These conferences, she says, "provided the child with the opportunity to articulate and demonstrate what they had learned within the context of their own work." She referred to her conferences as "sacred moments" that "enabled us to come to know one another on a personal level."

It is not until Whelan arrives at her last school that we start to gain a sense of the tensions between the story of school and Whelan's story to live by. It is here that the seams become apparent, and Whelan finds herself "at a crossroads." She names two possible stories: in one, her story to live by comes into tension with the stories of others and the story of school; in the other, she goes along with the plotline chosen by the rest of the staff. In Huber's case, there are two conflicting stories by which she could live out her teaching, stories she describes as being voices in her head. In Whelan's case, these two conflicting stories are made explicit through her use of the metaphor of diverging roads. In one story, the story of conferencing as reporting to parents and as an event separate from the making of curriculum conflicts with another, Whelan's story, a story of conferences as integral to curriculum making.

The depth with which Whelan's identity is wrapped up with her story of curriculum making is made apparent in her despair at giving up her story and conducting conferences that, for her, make her wonder about "what important parts of myself I leave behind on the trail." This is a teacher who fears losing her identity, her story to live by, and who finds herself "losing sight of who I am and what I know."

Nancy's Story

Nancy's identity, her story to live by, is that of a nurse educator working under what she sees are difficult working conditions: too small a classroom, too many students, too many languages, not enough time. Even with these difficulties there is a sense, after one's reading her biography as a student and nurse, that she has found herself in teaching.

Difficult conditions surface again and again in her story. For example, she found many parts of her own education difficult. Even as she studied for her university degree in nursing, educators were seen as dismissive of her nursing experience. Living a story of difficult working conditions was also her story of practicing nursing. When she left the general surgical unit early in her nursing career, she "felt that I wasn't giving enough to my patients," something she attributed to the staff shortages and difficult working conditions. She left nursing in search of a story to live by only to find that she missed nursing. She ultimately returned to nursing but in a different sort of place, a ship, where presumably, the working conditions would allow her more satisfying relationships with her patients. During this time she began to explore the connections between nurse and nurse educator.

Eventually she found herself living a story as a nurse educator where she works to "instill a love of nursing into my students" and where she says she emphasizes personal contact and anecdotal material to give students a sense of "the reality" of nursing. She wants to "instill a little bit more of the humanities, instead of making it all clinical."

As we try to unravel Nancy's identity, her story to live by, there appear to be two interconnected plotlines. In one, the plot is built around dissatisfaction with the formal nursing education process: the psychiatric nurse educator who disliked the subject matter; the lack of respect for students' experiences noted especially in her university degree program; the discrepancy between course theory and the practice of nursing, first noted in the chapter in her reflections on her experience as a student in psychiatric nursing. She follows this plotline as she tries to be a different kind of teacher in her relationship with students. She has students complete personal history questionnaires, tells them anecdotes from her own nursing practice, learns their names although there are large numbers, and reinforces what is important about being a nurse.

The second plotline is her search for a place within the nursing profession where she can live a satisfying story. She works in several different places, and repeatedly returns to pursue her own formal education until she eventually finds a story to live by in nursing education. She does not find a place of perfection here, because the difficult working circumstances that have followed her through nursing are present in the nursing education setting. What sustains both plotlines, and her story to live by, is her identity, which is bound up in her sense of the success of her students in passing their RN exams. It is enough for her to know that some students come back and say that, while writing their exams, they remember her teaching and are guided by her experience. These students' stories sustain her story to live by as a nurse educator in spite of the continuing difficult working situations.

Summary

So what do we make of these three stories of curriculum making? They are remarkably more complex than at first reading. As we look over the stories, we find curriculum and identity shaping each other in intricate ways. In one, Huber's story, we see a young teacher living out one story in her classroom place on the landscape, knowing that the story is in conflict with the way in which she is storied on the out-of-classroom place by her principal and other teachers. She struggles with this and maintains a cover story outside her classroom, which makes it possible for her to continue to live a certain story. However, it is done at a considerable price as she struggles with the tension between the mandated curriculum and the curriculum that, in the end, she feels she must teach. She continually questions her identity because both plotlines in her head are ones she believes she should live by. Yet, these are in conflict. She must choose, and does.

In Whelan's story we see a teacher who has a strong story to live by, in which teacher-parent-student conferences are part of her curriculum making. In the face of a different story of school Whelan eventually gives up her story, her identity, to "buckle under" and fit in with the story of school lived out by the school staff. Again, this conflict, and her resolution, comes at a huge price and she concludes by saying that she is "losing sight of who I am." Thus, while Huber knows two stories to live by that she must choose between, Whelan has only one and gives it up.

In Nancy's story we also see someone who has a story to live by and who runs into conflict in different working situations. She continues to search for a way to work in nursing that will allow her to live her story of it. She eventually finds a place in nursing education that, though it does not fulfill the conditions of her story to live by, creates the possibility for student response sufficient for her to continue. There is a struggle for identity as she describes what she cannot do because of the working conditions. Nevertheless, the intensity of her struggle as represented in the text is much less than is seen in Huber's and Whelan's cases. We might imagine that had the text focused on some of the more difficult times in Nancy's life as nurse practitioner that a different, perhaps more intense, identity story would have emerged.

We conclude this chapter with a strong sense of how teacher identities commingle on the professional knowledge landscape. There is nothing in the stories to suggest an inevitable conflict between conduit-prescribed curriculum and teacher identity. It would appear that for two of the people, Huber and Nancy, the prescribed curriculum is welcomed into and becomes part of their identities as teachers. Indeed, in both chapters, the identity conflicts—crisis in Huber's case—come from not being able to live out that conduit-prescribed story for reasons confronted in their working lives: in Huber's case because of her sense of student needs and her more strongly held communal story to live by, and in Nancy's case, because the working conditions make it difficult, if not impossible, to do all she wishes in terms of the prescribed curriculum.

One person, Whelan, lives a story in direct conflict with the prescribed curriculum. There is a sense in her chapter of the inexorability of the institutionalized conduit-prescribed story of curriculum. Whelan worries that she must give up her story to live by.

Taken over time there is a sense in Huber and Nancy's story of a mutual interaction between identity and prescribed curriculum, one with give-and-take along the way. On the other hand there is little sense of this in Whelan's case. She worries that she will lose her story to live by if she lives the prescribed story. It is evident that in all three cases, institutional stories are crucial influences on teachers' identity. It is also evident that each person responds in her own way to that institutional setting with dramatically different consequences for the place each occupies on the landscape and for how she views the relationship of the out-of-classroom place to the in-classroom place. Each person creates a special place and orientation that is given by her story to live by and that may be said to constitute her professional identity.

CHAPTER 9

Composing, Sustaining, and Changing Stories to Live By

So far in this book we have focused on the web of stories—teachers' stories, stories of teachers, school stories, stories of schools—that make up the landscape of schooling. We have used these terms to explore teachers' professional identity on the professional knowledge landscape. We have tried to show that teachers' working lives are shaped by stories and that these stories to live by compose teacher identity. These stories may be held to with conviction and tenacity. Modifications of them, implied or required by institutional life, can result in intensely felt dilemmas. People may have mixed feelings about their teaching, be critical of people and institutional policies and representatives, take issue and debate with their colleagues and, in extreme cases, resign and search for different employment where their identities, their stories to live by, may, in fact, be lived by. Whereas some stories are composed and sustained over time by being confirmed in various ways, other stories change to meet different institutional contexts. In this chapter we explore the composing, sustaining, and changing of stories to live by.

Composing a Story to Live By

"Who am I?" and "Who are you?" are common identity queries, queries that often imply a fixed identity as if somehow or other the answer to the question touched something rootlike at the core of a person's being. Versions of the therapeutic literature take for granted that getting in touch with the "real me/you" will reveal a solid base for meeting life with integrity. *Identity* is a term that tends to carry a burden of hard reality, something like a rock, a forest, an entity. Being true to this identity, being true to oneself, is often thought to be a virtue. Yet, from the narrative point of view, identities have histories. They are narrative constructions that take shape as life unfolds and that may, as narrative constructions are wont to do, solidify into a fixed entity, an unchanging narrative construction, or they may continue to grow and change. They may even be, indeed, almost certainly are, multiple depending on the life situations in which one finds oneself. It is also common to think that people are somehow or other different people at work from who they are at home or at a social gathering, with their children, and so on. The identities we have, the stories we live by, tend to show different facets depending on the situations in which we find ourselves. This is no less true for teachers in their professional knowledge landscapes. Different facets, different identities, can show up, be reshaped and take on new life in different landscape settings. Both sides of this general picture are true in some measure: identities, the stories we live by, are, it would seem, not easily changed, so difficult, at times, it may appear that they are, indeed, fixed unchanging entities. But, as even the few stories in these chapters show, identities both have origins and change. It is our task in the following paragraphs to provide modest demonstration for these observations and to explore the conditions under which identities are composed, sustained, and changed.

We learn little of the origins of several of the participants' stories to live by in the six chapters. Huber as author/teacher begins her school year with a story to live by. Rose as author/principal begins his administration with an idea for a changed story of school for teachers and students to live by. Still, with imagination, and were this not a metalevel text, we might return to discussions with these two people with an eye towards exploring the origins of the assumed identities. In other participant cases, there are some hints that provide clues to the origins of the stories lived by.

The evidential hints for the origins of participant identities are seen in various aspects of their lives: Whelan in her school life, Nancy in her professional education and again in her nursing life, Sara in her home life and again in her teaching life, and in Davies's chapter of the relationship of teachers to the history of things made in their school. The stories as told are partially observational and partially based on memory.

There is little in the chapters to indicate the status of these memories nor how they are remembered, whether as correspondence, memory boxes, family stories, journals, and so on. Many of our memories have this quality. We remember events of many years ago as if they happened today, or so it feels. We remember details and experience emotion. Much has intervened and, undoubtedly, events as happened and as remembered are only loosely connected factually but strongly connected narratively. The memory now, of the event then, is intimately tied to the narrative paths we have followed. And although we may mistrust the veracity of the memory as an empirical record, we celebrate it as a revealing narrative construction. This is how we read all of the chapters and it is on this basis that we construct our metalevel text on the composing, sustaining, and changing of personal professional identity.

The Formation of Whelan's Identity

The origins of Whelan's identity in her school life are mostly shrouded, though passionate moments provide revealing hints. There is little to suggest where her embodied journey metaphor comes from. For the reader it is simply there. But her sense of relationship to children and, in particular, her growing commitment to student-led conferences as components of her journey as teacher, show up as a developing story to live by. Her overall story begins in year 1 with spirited, hope-filled preparations for her first class, and concludes with her story 7 years later with fears of losing herself and of not knowing who she is. In the intervening years, the formation of her professional identity occurred, which made possible the story lived out in year 7. For Whelan, the basis for the development of these aspects of her identity are seen in the enthusiasm and hope in her planning and in her warm, relational observations of the early days of her teaching. She describes the things that she did with her students, referring to her place as "tucked away in our special classroom with our door shut to the outside world," and she goes on to say, "Together, we were building a magical place and we were happy." Happiness is a powerful force and must surely have colored her sense of what it meant to be a teacher. The contrast between this happiness and the letdown in March when she conducted the "unfulfilling" interviews with parents, leaving her tired and relieved that they were over, appears to have created a tension of the sort that Schön (1983) describes as driving professional practice. Whelan describes her classroom experiences as magical and happy and her March conferences as tiring, unfulfilling, and sad. Her situation, her place on the landscape, is clearly taking hold and shaping her identity as a teacher. It is not only that she is likely to create an identity associated with happy and pleasant circumstances, and not with sad and tiring ones, but also that the tension between the two creates a positive force for rethinking, and extending her story to live by with respect to the unsatisfactory conference experience.

Whelan changed schools that year and found herself in a situation that appears to have confirmed the circumstances that led to a happy, magical classroom the year before. But now it is no longer only her "tucked-away special classroom," it is also the story of school. In effect, as she saw it, it was the school identity. Reading her passages on her second school, there is a blending in which she fully becomes part of the story of school. Thus, the circumstances of her happy, formative, secluded classroom of the 1st year are expanded to a communal setting in her 2nd year of teaching. She had constructed a satisfying classroom story to live by in her 1st year. But this was, undoubtedly, a fragile story, an identity only partly molded and in the making. Time and again in this book, and in other writings, we have noted the disparity between classroom stories to live by and stories of school and of teachers that conflict with these classroom stories to live by and that result in cover stories. What a powerful formative moment it must have been, then, for Whelan to discover that the things she enjoyed and what she was coming to believe about herself as a teacher were valued throughout the school by her colleagues. The doubts that one might imagine a beginning teacher to have about possible discrepancies between what she lives and what is valued on the out-of-classroom place on her landscape evaporated for Whelan at her second school. Moreover, the story of school in her second school led teachers to treat parent conferences in a way that washed away the troubling conditions of the March experience the year before. From the point of view of Whelan's identity formation, it would appear that the conditions in her second school were, therefore, doubly influential: They communally confirmed Whelan's heretofore secret stories of classroom teaching and they wiped away what appears to have been the one serious blight on Whelan's 1st year of teaching. Her emerging story of conferences was written large in the new school, where two special teachers "guided me forward on my journey, and helped me find a process that felt just right" and where "children were the focal point and the key communicators as they celebrated their learning and growth with their parents and teachers." Although she does not say so, one might imagine that Whelan was finding the words, phrases, and reasoning at her second school to support her somewhat undifferentiated feelings about what should be done in student conferences. Her second school provided, at one and the same time, communal support and theoretical underpinnings for Whelan's developing story to live by.

Our metalevel reading of her text suggests that these first 2 years were the central times in the formation of Whelan's identity as a teacher. There is a sense of awe, of spirituality, as she tries to express in words her experience with the child Sarah and what this means for her sense of identity.

Her subsequent years at her second school and her year at the third appear to have been a period of continued confirmation and sustenance of her story to live by. Undoubtedly, were the reader privy to more detail, to day-by-day, moment-to-moment field records, formative nuances would be noticed. But, as the story is told, what we see as readers is confirmation and expression of Whelan's newly constructed teacher identity. The year at her third school no doubt provided significant strengthening because this was not a year of clear sailing: it was one in which a new staff came together in a new building and took charge of their curriculum planning. Whelan played a key role in developing the school policy on "communicating student growth" because of her experience in the previous years. Shadows appear. The Grade 7 but not the Grades 8 and 9 teachers decide to proceed in a way consistent with Whelan's story to live by. It is clear that she is aware of the clouds but adopts yet another story to live by that makes the clouds non-threatening for her identity. It was a story of different strokes for different folks. She said it "became a place where diversity in style was celebrated."

The remainder of the chapter, and of her teaching years, are ones in which this corollary story breaks down, and the school staff, through their own democratic means, decide as a total school to pursue one pattern of conference. There is one more year of respite at a new school where individual teachers "were free to go with the style of conferencing which best suited us and our children" but, she writes, "From there we move to a locked-in format in which we would run personal conferences in November and open-house conferences in March."

It is fascinating to read the counter story from this period on in light of the developing story up to this point. The year of respite turned out, in fact, as she wrote about it, to be a year of competition. The communal atmosphere that had dominated her second school and, it would appear, the diverse paths taken in her third school now led to strain. Though it is not strongly in evidence, it would appear that Whelan goes through a period of self-doubt when her identity, however marginally, comes into question. Still, the predominant picture that emerges is that Whelan's identity, mostly fixed by her 2nd or perhaps 3rd year of teaching, no longer develops, placing her in a tense situation where an alternative story to live by, and the conditions it creates, do not support her identity. It would be fascinating to pick up this story some years into the future and to see whether Whelan's identity has remained firm or whether it has yet again changed with changing circumstances.

Composing and Sustaining Other Stories to Live By

The remaining five chapters in this set of six reveal additional personal and professional conditions under which professional identity is formed and sustained. Readers may find it profitable to unpack the research texts contained in the four chapters and to construct their own metalevel accounts of the sort we have provided for Whelan. In the following paragraphs we sketch the broad outlines of our reading of these texts in terms of identity formation and sustenance and we draw attention to special points of interest not seen in our account of Whelan's text.

In Quan, Phillion, and He's chapter we are privy to Nancy's story of a large segment of her life, from her days as a nursing student to her current work as a nursing educator. There are very few hints in Nancy's story of how some aspects of her story to live by were formed. The outlines of two significant parts of her story are, however, dimly visible. Her sense of herself as someone who connects with students at a personal level with personal and professional/practical anecdotes appears, in the eyes of the chapter authors, to be connected to her ongoing struggles with what and how she was taught in her own education. She believes that it is important for students to know "what really happens out there and this is how you can deal with it" and in the process she wants to "instill a love of nursing into my students without them hating the educational process." This stance toward her students is in direct contrast to her own education where, for example, she believes that her own background and knowledge were ignored when she returned, at age 27, to a university degree program and was required to take high school courses. She said, "they treated me like I had no brains at all . . . your diploma does not mean much." It would, we think, be fascinating to explore this story in more depth. It appears that embedded in Nancy's story to live by is, perhaps, a more forceful, though mostly unseen, story of her place, and the place of nursing, in the world of theory and practice. Quan, Phillion, and He write that "reflecting on her psychiatric experiences with a student, she realized that she had disliked the theoretical component but had enjoyed working with psychiatric patients." Thus, a story of experience and its place in nursing and nursing education, and the values attached to stories of different placements as nursing student, nurse, and nurse educator would, we believe, be revealing of the formation of Nancy's story to live by.

This story, this possible, we imagine, element in Nancy's identity might also be significant in what appears to be another developmental aspect of Nancy's identity over the years. There is a sense in her earlier years of a strong, unchanging identity that put her in conflict with institutional stories. She did, after all, leave nursing when the conditions did not support what she felt should be done in a general surgical unit. When the reader picks up Nancy's story in her teaching there is more of a sense of doing what one can under the circumstances, a sense that the rocklike identity that we imagine may have been at work earlier has grown and changed to one where the same story to live by, the same identity, is maintained but expressed more flexibly depending on the circumstances. To the extent that this is a meaningful reading of Nancy's identity formation over the years it is suggestive of Nancy's shifting place in a story of theory and practice.

Interesting aspects of the development of Sara's identity seen in Rose's chapter, and of the teachers in the school written about by Davies, are evident in their respective chapters. Sara's professional identity can be traced to the way in which she leads her personal life. Rose repeatedly remarks on the parallels between Sara's personal and professional school life. Furthermore, as with Whelan, it is clear that Sara's sense of identity is sustained, in important measure, communally, by other teachers and by a principal who shares and strengthens her story to live by. There appears to be a spider web of influences that contain and sustain Whelan's and Sara's identities. Although we have little relevant data, we might imagine that there are childhood and family stories kept emotionally alive through tellings, retellings, and givings back by family and friends. There are trusted professional colleagues, such as Rose for Sara, who value and reinterpret these stories and a way of living in positive moral ways. Such response is surely a powerful identity-sustaining influence for Sara.

The teachers in Davies's story provide, in part, quite a different insight into the formation of teacher identity. On the one hand, communal aspects are again important, as groups of teachers come together to resist the changes being brought about by the principal to the hallways, library, and gymnasium. As the story unfolds, it is clear that the teachers and community members, some no longer associated with the school, figure as a strong communal force, having been involved in the development of the original work. From this it would appear that communal sustenance for teacher identity can reside in memory in the past as well as currently among colleagues.

What is quite different in Davies's story is the role that things may play in the formation of teacher identity. The things, banners and logos, thrown out and painted over, were not merely things. They were materialized memories, repositories of shared experience. The teachers in Davies's school had a strong relationship to these things. These relationships, relationships of the imagination, confirmed communally with colleagues, sustained Davies's teachers' stories to live by. This sustenance was central to the new principal's intended changes in this school.

Changing Stories to Live By

We understand schools as a landscape of interacting stories that bear directly on teacher identity and, by association, on teacher satisfaction with their work. These matters are at the heart, we believe, of the theory, policy, and practice of school change and improvement. From the point of view of the ideas presented in this book, school change is the creation of new stories to live by. School stability is the sustenance of stories being lived by. The often cited resistance of teachers to school change is, in our terms, a question of teacher identity and of the conditions under which stories to live by are sustained and new stories to live by are composed. In our terms, teacher resistance is the maintenance of a story to live by in the face of school change.

Change, the creation of new stories to live by, may originate with individual practitioners, as it does with Huber and her changing afternoon curriculum, or it may have its origins in the out-of-classroom place on the landscape as institutionally sanctioned new stories enter the landscape via the conduit. Rose's and Davies's chapters illustrate this latter source. Change may, as we show below, arise communally as groups of people pursue practical inquiries.

This problem of change is more complex than it might first appear. Where do new stories to live by come from? What are the origins of change? Rose's own story, his story of himself as a new principal, helps us think this through. Rose comes to Briardon School with a new story of school. At one point he finds himself in a gymnasium with his entire student body. Part of his story is the importance of listening to student voices in school planning. In contrast to the school story already in place, he, for the first time, calls a meeting of all students. The reason for calling the meeting, and the way in which he begins to conduct the meeting, is essentially an attempt to live out his story. From this point of view it is a more or less straightforward implementation activity. The story is quickly interrupted when a student says, "If you really want to help us, then get us a real lunchroom." This leads to an after-school work party where Rose and a group of students knock down concrete school walls without board approval. On the one hand, this is consistent with Rose's story, since it does represent listening to student voices. But it also makes Rose exceedingly uncomfortable. He knows as an administrator that he is also to live a story of conformity with board policy and procedure. He knows full well that he has crossed a line and now finds himself living a conflicting story. The point we wish to make with this, however, is that it is also a change, a creative development, in Rose's own story to live by. He surely did not begin his implementation attempts with the idea that he would change his own story of school. He intended to change others' stories of Briardon School. Nor did he set out to challenge the conduit. Yet he quickly found himself on the margins and in conflict.

What is interesting to us is what this incident shows about how school stories and individual practitioners' stories are changed. In much of our work we have seen how stories to live by are communally sustained as people support one another through confirmation of their beliefs, values, and actions and as they share stories and recollections. We have paid less attention to how new stories are composed communally. The same communal forces that act to sustain a story may, as well, act communally to create new stories to live by. This event in Briardon School shows not only how communities may originate new stories to live by but how this might be done. In this case Rose, in calling a student assembly, is living out a story to live by. It becomes an action setting where problems are addressed. Confirmation is not the issue. Indeed the opposite is the case as students challenge Rose to make good on his promises. Rose bends and alters his ideas as he and the students, both that day and in subsequent ones, work through a possible resolution of the problem posed by the students. At the same time that Rose's story is modified in the inquiry, his story is strengthened and, we well imagine, his sense of identity as principal is strengthened. It is not as if he tossed aside one story and created a new one; instead, he evolved a new story that placed him in conflict with the conduit.

Before we leave this point it is important to note that when teachers come together and share stories, new stories to live by can also be composed. We see this later in Rose's chapter when Sara works with Clark, John, and Kay to compose a new story to live by in their learning community. Our account of change and stability is not intended to place value on one over the other. It may be valuable to communally confirm and stabilize a school story to live by. It may be valuable to communally create a new story to live. However, it is equally plausible that either, or both, of these stories are undesirable. Furthermore, depending on how one is positioned on the landscape in relation to the stories, the person may, or may not, value the stories.

Summary

In this chapter we examined the stories presented in Chapters 2 to 7 to explore the conditions under which stories to live by are composed and sustained and the conditions under which new stories to live by are introduced and interact with existing stories to live by. We reviewed elements of change and stability in schools and in teacher identity. Why is it, and what makes it possible, for some teachers and practitioners to hold tenaciously to a story to live by when confronted with a landscape of conflicting stories? And why is it that some new stories to live by, some newly introduced out-of-classroom changes, are successful in some cases and thwarted in others? We do not, of course, come up with universal answers to these questions. We do show how intimately connected school change and stability are to teacher identity and to what one might call the archaeology of school landscapes. Every landscape needs to be "dug" in its own right. With a knowledge of the narrative history of school stories and of the central stories to live by for teachers and others in the school, we believe that it is at least possible to understand and plan for change in a way that is sensitive to the question of who we are as practitioners.

CHAPTER 10

Borders of Space and Time

As Chapter 9 ended we noted the need to pay attention to the nature of school landscapes as akin to archaeological sites. As we thought about this, we realized that one of the common features of professional knowledge landscapes is their borders.

We argued earlier in the book that we saw the landscape as composed of different places—the in-classroom place and the out-of-classroom place. Because we see teachers' lives as being lived out on both places on the landscape, we see teachers as crossing borders between these two places many times each day. Earlier, we wrote of the dilemmas they experience as they move between these two places. Teachers also cross a border as they consider how their actions will be storied by others outside their in-classroom places. In this sense, teachers create imagined border-crossings. Huber's concern about how she might be storied by her administrator and other teachers were they to learn of what she did in her teaching is an instance of such an imagined border-crossing.

We made it clear that there are many out-of-classroom places on the landscape—out-of-classroom offices, hallways, staff rooms, board offices, other district offices, and so forth. There are also out-of-classroom places where teachers, children, and parents live, places that we earlier called personal landscapes.

A landscape metaphor helps us to see the possibility of borders that divide aspects of professional knowledge. There are borders, dividers, spaces that demarcate one place from another. We wrote in Chapter 1 about the kind of knowledge found in each place on the landscape.

In schools, these borders, these places on the landscape, are made institutionally, and respected by the individuals who live their stories out within the institutions. Indeed, for most individuals, they are so taken for granted,

so embodied in one's sense of living on the landscape, that they are not noticed. It is only when someone is new to the landscape or when something
has changed about the landscape that we awaken to the borders. When new
policies are enacted that somehow threaten the borders, threaten to change
the nature of knowledge within each place on the landscape, or both, we
become most awake to borders.

Borders mark the dividing places. Borders say that something different
is about to begin. Things pass across the border and different things happen
to them. Different things are important on different sides of the border. Things
get across the border in different ways. There is a history to everything that
happens on each side of the border. Borders themselves have histories. There
are ways that permit things to pass the border and ways that things are treated
on either side of the border.

In addition to being spatial, borders can be temporal. We have, in other
places, shown that schools are organized cyclically and that these cycles give
rise to experiential rhythms, ways of experiencing professional life in more
or less aesthetic and satisfying ways. In the following, we briefly summarize
our account of the importance of time in school life. That argument, however, preceded our inquiry into the professional knowledge landscape and
we shall, therefore, revisit these ideas with an eye toward the role of temporality in establishing borders on professional knowledge landscapes. We will
show how time and professional identity are linked.

In our study of the cyclic temporal structure of schooling (Connelly &
Clandinin, 1990a, 1993) we remarked that schools are ruled by the clock on
a daily basis and by promotion on an annual basis. Annual and daily cycles
reflect in some complex way more general social cycles, some of which are
natural, such as the seasons, and some of which are conventional, such as
the yearly calendar. Looking inward at the workings of the school reveals
grand epicycles such as primary, junior, intermediate, and senior divisions
within a 12-year cycle of schooling. Also revealed are more miniature cycles
such as the 6-day school cycle and the duty cycles of teachers. We have discussed at least 10 school cycles: annual, holiday, monthly, weekly, 6-day, duty,
day, teacher, report, and within-class cycles. There are undoubtedly others.
These cycles not only vary in duration but can also vary according to sequence, temporal location, and rate of occurrence. Cycles of a certain duration, therefore, determine a characteristic sequence of events, at a certain point
in time, and at a certain rate of occurrence. For instance, the school 6-day
cycle orders the temporal reality of different groups of participants, students,
teachers, principal and support staff, in school over a succession of 6 day
periods. That is, what may appear on a curriculum planner's desk as a linear
temporal structure of schooling is experienced by teachers and others as a

cyclic temporal order. Time, and therefore the idea of rhythm in the narrative of teaching, is fundamentally based on a complex of interacting cycles.

We showed how the cycles had a grip on people's professional lives and, when challenged or transgressed, the rhythms of teaching—that is, the sense of satisfaction and appropriateness of teaching—is interrupted. For instance, in our work at Bay Street School a provincial mandate required an additional 22 minutes daily of school time. That additional instructional time meant that the afternoon would need to be interrupted with an afternoon recess break and that teachers needed to develop new rhythms around late afternoon teaching. Furthermore, the later school dismissal time interrupted the cycle of professional development and school governance activities. Teachers had a great deal of difficulty accommodating to these changes, struggling to find ways to use the instructional time block after recess. After-school cabinet meetings were moved to a later start time and teachers experienced disruption in their school-leaving time. There was a great deal of staff discussion over these matters. The disruption experienced by school personnel would appear, to an unknowing observer, to be out of proportion to the small amount of additional required time. We argued that the meaning of the staff's response was due to the interruption in the cycles. A series of interacting temporal cycles was affected. Teachers' rhythmic knowing of the school day was profoundly affected.

These cycles, we now realize, create temporal borders. It might seem that it would be easier to cross, or to alter, a cyclic temporal border than to cross or alter a spatial border. Spatial borders tend to be visible to the eye, often demarcated with walls and doors. Temporal borders are in the mind and on paper on the timetable. But, as our study of time in schools with reported incidents such as that just described for Bay Street School taught us, temporal cycles are linked to the rhythmic experience of schooling and are crossed or modified with great difficulty. Given that we know that teacher knowledge is embodied and carries with it moral, emotional, and aesthetic dimensions, the difficulty of crossing and modifying borders is not surprising. A very large part of a school's moral and ethical life is constructed around adherence to temporal cycles and to the maintenance of their temporal borders. Teachers who do not start their classes on time, or students who come late, are judged to be not only in violation of school rules but morally wanting: lazy, inconsiderate of others, selfish, incompetent.

It is clear that these moral qualities, and the aesthetic and emotional dimensions to which we refer, have a great deal to do with teachers' senses of self, their identity, their stories to live by. For instance, a teacher in one of our studies, Stevenson (1989), moved from a semestered Grade 7–12 school with 90-minute class periods to a nonsemestered Grade 7–9 school with 42-

minute class periods. Prior to the move, Stevenson described herself as a self-confident teacher. Within a short time in the new school she was, in her words, "totally distraught over my inability to be the kind of teacher that I knew how to be." The changed temporal borders that define her rhythmic knowing caused her to question her story of herself as an effective teacher. She found herself wondering, "With my timetable in front of me, why could I not begin to organize my days according to where I had to be and when I had to be there?" Without transforming the story to live by as she crossed from one set of temporal borders to another she brought her teacher identity into question. Confidence was replaced with doubt.

We now turn to a detailed analysis of spatial and temporal borders.

Spatial Borders

As Rose begins his chapter, we see him clearly situated on the out-of-classroom place on the landscape. As a principal new to a school with a school plotline of "toughness and violence," he is hiring new teachers. He has already begun to interrupt the story of school being lived out by doing some unexpected things such as working with students to knock down walls. These interruptions on the out-of-classroom place on the landscape have already begun to change the story of school being lived out. They served as a kind of warning from him that the story of school which storied the students as unsuccessful was unacceptable to him. This new story of school that he wants to compose is being expressed as he hires new teachers, and he is awake to it as he interviews Sara and as he tells us the story of their first meeting. He relates that he "was determined to recruit teachers whose teacher stories featured an understanding of relationship as central to student learning."

As he tells Sara's story, we learn that she begins teaching with a clear border between her in-classroom place and the out-of-classroom places. She "worked in isolation from other professionals" in her classroom place and lived out the demands placed on her from the out-of-classroom place. But even in this first year, we learn that Sara has begun to test the flexibility of the borders. We learn that she begins to feel "comfortable" in out-of-classroom places with Rose, her principal, and with the teachers in the next double-station classroom. Rose, already with a firm sense of wanting a new story of school that featured children with the possibility of living success stories, had begun to foster the breaking down of the borders between teachers' in-classroom places. Sara begins to play with the borders between her in-classroom place and those of other teachers with whom she has a developing relationship.

There is an interesting transition and shift in the borders. As the teachers begin to form into learning communities with larger groups of students, the borders around in-classroom places begin to reform, so that they exist around the larger learning communities. There are still borders around the in-classroom places, but teachers agreed to give up their borders around each individual classroom. Borders remain, but there are fewer of them. The story of school became one of five different learning communities, each separated from the other learning communities by the stories that were lived out in them. In other places, Rose describes the ways that the out-of-classroom places between the learning communities created a kind of maze for students to negotiate. The students moved among out-of-classroom places where hats were or were not allowed, food was or was not allowed, and so on. Clearly, the out-of-classroom place was a no person's land as the borders around the learning communities took hold.

But within Sara's learning community the borders had all but disappeared. There were no longer physical borders within the big room. Nor were there borders between different subject matter knowledges, as the teachers no longer lived the specialist knowledge story. Nor were the borders holding firm between teachers' lives outside of school and their in-school lives, as we learned from the weekend planning experience. Bernie, one of the teachers, struggles to maintain this border between his personal and his school life as he wonders if the planning will fill his whole life space. In the end even Bernie lets his border go, or so it seems, as he says that the experience was "one of the greatest years of teaching in my career." The borders between students' out-of-school and in-school lives also began to become more permeable as students brought their stories to school; food became available; tired students could sleep; out-of-school interests became part of the in-school curriculum; space became available to them in out-of-school time before and after school; and space became available to them when they no longer attended the school; and so on.

The borders between teachers' lives and those of their students also began to blur as teachers ate lunch with students and became involved with students' lives. Some of these borders are apparent in the shift to the new story of school, but they again come into sharp relief as still another story of school is put into place with the principal who succeeds Rose. He wanted to have one story of school dominant in the whole school and he began to try to bring the five distinct learning communities together into the same story of school. It is not made clear what his preferred story of school was, but it is clear that, as he begins to work toward that one story, the borders that had begun to be more permeable in Sara's learning community were now storied as borders that had been transgressed. As the chapter is written, we see the borders of specialist knowledge be reestablished; we see the borders of the

close teacher/student/student relationships established over 3 years of working together be reshaped into the more established one-year relationship;
we see the borders of special education and regular education students be
strengthened, and so on.

In Davies's chapter, we learn still more about the borders that shape the
landscape and, as they do so, shape the stories that teachers live on the landscape. We accompany Davies to a school and watch with her as the out-of-
classroom place is changed through the removal of some school banners and
decorations. A new principal has arrived at the school and he begins to change
the physical appearance of the out-of-classroom place, perhaps with the intent to indicate a new story of school.

The teachers mostly watch in silence until Davies, as researcher, begins
to make a space for a conversation about the disappearing banners. It is here
that we learn something more about borders on the professional knowledge
landscape. The teachers had not spoken of the banners, even though many
of them felt strongly about them. In their silence, there seemed to be an acceptance that the out-of-classroom place belonged to the principal. The border between in-classroom and out-of-classroom places indicated that he
owned the out-of-classroom place. When Davies asked the question, she
learned that the teachers were uncertain about how to bring up the topic.
There seemed to be no space for such conversation about the principal's new
story of school. Taking down the banners was one expression of this new
story and it appeared that the teachers had learned that they were to expect
change with a new principal. Furthermore, they seemed to accept that change
was a good thing, not to be questioned. They were not to question that the
new principal had been brought in to change the school and that one of the
borders on the professional knowledge landscape, that is, the border that separated in-classroom from out-of-classroom, meant that he could change the out-
of-classroom "decor" without their involvement. They saw the entrance hall
as "nobody's space." Davies describes Jeff and Ellen, two teachers, as silenced
and needing the safety of their in-classroom places in order to be able to speak
about what they saw happening. Davies describes them as feeling that it would
be unprofessional to speak out on the out-of-classroom place.

Davies's chapter draws attention to the questions of borders as they demarcate the physical territory in school. Who owns various places in schools?
Do teachers "own" their in-classroom places and administrators own the hallways, staff rooms, school main offices, and so on? Do school specialists own
gymnasiums, libraries, and so on? In Davies's chapter, the questions of borders and what that might imply for ownership come to the fore.

In Whelan's chapter we see other issues of borders on the professional
knowledge landscape. Whelan lives her story of curriculum making as one
that brings teacher, students, and parents together in carefully thought-

through conferences that for her are moments when children share their stories of experience of their time in Whelan's classroom. In some ways, as did Sara, she wants to blur the borders between the personal landscapes of herself and students and their parents. She does this, in part, by deliberately trying to import the home into the classroom. She wants parents to be part of the children's education and she works to create situations where that is possible, such as parent-student-teacher conferences.

Whelan knows that the border between home and school is very real, for she learned that in her first school. However, she also knows that it is a border that can be transgressed, for she lived that story in her second school. But she understands that she needs to continually work to blur the border not only with other staff members at her school, but with the parents of the students with whom she works. She does not give this latter border much attention in her chapter as she turns to the difficulty of blurring the border in her own classroom in tension with other teachers and her administrator in her last school. She realizes that she must do something very different in order for parents to be part of the curriculum making that she and the children are doing in the classroom; she wants the parents and the children there.

Temporal Borders

In the set of chapters under consideration the most striking influence of temporal borders on teachers' sense of identity is seen in Rose's chapter. At one point in Rose's tenure as principal, there is no master timetable for the school. These are the most common temporal organizers in junior and senior high schools, setting the length of individual subject matter periods, the number of periods in the day, what subjects and activities follow one another, and so on. A glance at the timetable tells a knowledgeable school person what any one teacher or child is doing at any given time of the day. Nowadays, authorized school visitors in search of a particular child will be handed a computer-generated schedule for the child based on a master timetable. This master timetable creates almost impenetrable boundaries. A child and a teacher have to be in a specific place, studying a specific subject at specified times. Interesting class discussions, school activities, or events cannot carry over beyond the block of time assigned for that activity; otherwise everyone is thrown into disarray. Furthermore, the master timetable is carefully built around the curriculum-mandated time allotments for each subject matter. Blocks of time are assigned to teachers considered to be specialists in a subject matter area. Teachers tell a story of themselves as subject matter teachers. From an identity point of view the master timetable is, therefore, directly associated with teachers' stories to live by, their identity of themselves as professionals.

The lack of a master timetable in Rose's school was, therefore, a major breech in temporal order and must have come with considerable negotiation around an alternate temporal ordering. The alternate temporal order, we learn, was associated with learning communities where teams of teachers spent all day with particular groups of students. Although Rose does not focus his writing on identity issues, there are hints of this in his account of the difficulties experienced by Sara's learning community team. The story this team lives by is one of its members being in relationship with one another and with students in the community. The teachers who worked in Sara's learning community composed stories to live by around community and relationship with students. As they lived out these stories, they transgressed many other temporal borders as they allowed students to come in early and stay late, eat their lunch with their teachers in the big room, as they planned to stay with a group of students for 3 years and, of course, as they broke down all of the cycles associated with subject matter.

The community began its year with 60 excess students, according to the school's approved formula. After a month of negotiation the community was given two options: one was to redistribute the excess students to other learning communities; the second was to accept part-time subject matter specialists in lieu of full time teachers. Sara's group chose the second option because the first violated their relationship story to live by. Fragments of specialist teacher time were assigned.

It seems remarkable to us how far the teachers in this learning community would go to sustain their story to live by. Taking on 60 extra students is a huge commitment. It is not only a question of the workload they were prepared to take on—one has to wonder also at how the teacher union might have perceived this action. Choosing to keep the extra students is particularly remarkable considering that the teachers and students had only been together for a month. Yet, on the basis of their story to live by and the relationships established, they were even prepared to transgress union expectations.

Taking on fragments of teacher time had the result of forcing the learning community into following the master timetable based on subject matter specialties and their attendant blocks of time. As Rose writes, "The integrated, interdisciplinary, team-teaching and cooperative learning aspects of her (Sara's) story were severely constrained as flexibility was lost and control of time was subtly relocated on the out-of-classroom place through a master timetable."

What was going on at this point was that the temporal boundaries associated with subject matter were reintroduced and began to assert their control as borders. Specialist teachers had to be scheduled in and out of the learning community. The community's temporal cycles were dictated by the arrival and departure of the part-time subject matter specialists.

In this learning community, there were, then, two groups of teachers, each with different stories to live by and driven by different temporal borders. For the specialist teachers, their stories to live by were set by their subject matter specialties and their attendant borders associated with the school's master time-table. For Sara and her team of teachers their stories to live by were relational with a set of temporal borders associated with the holistic way they organized their annual curriculum. In Rose's chapter we learn nothing about the sense of rhythm obtained by the specialist teachers. However, we do learn that, for Sara, the arrangement was unaesthetic and morally wrong. It was the opposite of rhythmic. It was fragmented, disjointed, noncommunitarian, and nonrelational. The depth of Sara's unhappiness about the compromises in her story to live by are evident throughout Rose's chapter.

We see something similar in Whelan's chapter. We earlier made the point that identity issues in and around her attempt to create parent-teacher-student conferences were conceptual ones. Her story of curriculum was that conferences were an integral part of the ongoing curriculum making process. For other teachers we imagine that conference reporting was outside curriculum. It was a time to report on what had happened in the curriculum but not part of it. What we now want to do is to work through the temporal consequences of these different curricular stories to live by.

To remind readers, Whelan saw the conferences as a time when there was further learning as children described their school experiences to their parents and to their teacher. Conferences were culminations and turnover points in her overall curricular making. In order for her to express this concept of curriculum she needed to meet with parents on evenings and on weekends. These times became a part of her curriculum. The other teachers in Whelan's last school, who saw reporting as outside of curriculum, wanted to report to parents in the most efficient way. This was supported by the principal who took the view that teachers were already heavily committed and should minimize any extra work. Evening and weekend reporting meetings were, because they were extra curricular and therefore extra work, to be kept to a minimum.

What is going on here is that the different concepts of curriculum, the different curricular stories to live by, give rise to different temporal borders. For the other teachers in Whelan's last school, the curriculum fit temporally within the regular daily cycle as normally conceived. The time for parent conferences was additional, a minicycle to be composed of only a few evening meetings. To make these meetings a major part of their activity disrupted all sorts of other temporal borders. For example, being at school on a weekend interrupted the 5-day work-week cycle and its attendant personal and private cycles. As with most teachers, we imagine that these teachers engaged in marking and lesson planning during this private evening and weekend time. All of these matters are thrown off with too many evening and weekend meetings. For Whelan, on the other hand, these conferences were part and parcel of her curriculum. They established a major temporal border around which her other activities fit. Her alternative concept of curriculum, to which she was so strongly committed, carried with it a radically different set of temporal borders. In our view, it is clear that the strong attachment to these stories to live by, attachments which to an outside observer may appear overly strong, is more than merely conceptual. We saw this in Bay Street School with the small amount of added time to the daily cycle: we see it in Rose's chapter with Sara as she chooses to keep extra students, and it reappears in Whelan's strong attachment to her parent-student-teacher conferences.

Whelan's chapter highlights yet another point. The reaction of the other teachers to Whelan's conference reporting plan seems unduly strong. They insist, through democratic means, on selecting one approach for everyone. As readers we wonder about this insistence on a common approach. Initially, Whelan was able to live out her alternative story. In the 2nd year, doing the same thing, the school voted to prevent Whelan from having conferences that fit her story to live by. We wonder why the teachers changed. Why is it that what was a competing story in the 1st year has now become a conflicting story to be democratically chosen for or against? We think that part of the reason lies in the strength of attachment to the temporal borders and to the morality people see associated with them. To extend the temporal borders as Whelan did was to "rate break": to transgress the norms for, as some might think, the purpose of gaining parental favour. On this view, the other teachers are best understood as having composed a story of Whelan as someone who is trying to "get ahead," an identity story of career advancement. But Whelan's story of herself, her story to live by, is one rooted in her narrative experience of curriculum making. We do not in the least intend to imply that these other teachers acted out of malice. We believe that they were expressing a sense of professional morality born of a temporally defined sense of identity. Because rate breaking implies a moral judgement, it might even be argued that the teachers who voted to prevent Whelan from conducting conferences as she wished were actually voting to protect her from herself, something like a parent requiring something of a child for his or her own good although it hurts.

Borders and Stories to Live By

As we come to the end of this chapter we see that matters of professional identity are intimately interwoven with spatial and temporal borders on the professional knowledge landscape. We see that conceptual matters such as teachers' conceptions of curriculum or of a particular subject matter are important to understanding professional life on the landscape; however, in addition, people's experience, their personal practical knowledge, of space and time gives life force to their identity, to their stories to live by. Their stories to live by are more than the conceptual knowledge of curriculum, teaching, subject matter and so on. They are expressions of an embodied knowledge of the landscape, of space and time, of borders, cycles, and rhythms. They express an aesthetic sense of being in the right place at the right time and of doing certain things according to satisfying temporal cycles. They express a sense of moral appropriateness of certain actions associated with spatial and temporal borders and how people position themselves on the landscape relative to these borders.

People's stories to live by have moral, emotional, and aesthetic qualities. So too does the landscape. The preceding chapters show the possibility of tension and conflict as these stories to live by interact with the landscape.

CHAPTER 11

Stories to Live By: Teacher Identities on a Changing Professional Knowledge Landscape

As we look out on the world from our vantage point of sabbatical leaves, one in Toronto and one in Edmonton, we see the familiar world of schools and teaching in a state of transition, flux, even, it seems, radical change. As we pause and view this world we have a sense of uncertainty. What does this changing world mean for the stories we live by as teachers and teacher educators? Our feeling is that what we knew how to do well may no longer make sense for what we were doing it for. What good is what we know about teachers' knowledge if this is expressed in completely and dramatically different environments from those we have studied? What good is our way of thinking about teachers' lives, and the preparation of teachers for professional lives of teaching, if those lives are changing?

We feel unease, uncertainty, about how to continue to work in meaningful ways with teachers, with teacher educators, with graduate students preparing for lives of reflection on teaching. Who are we in this process, people who have heretofore been given an identity in educational research and teacher education by virtue of a certain kind of educational world? Where do we stand as we survey this educational world?

But even as we ask these questions we mistrust our very sense of uncertainty. How can we know what is happening? And, if we cannot, what trust do we put in our sense that there are, indeed, dramatic changes? Do we trust our emotional responses to the uncertainty and use them as guides for changing our identities as teacher educators and educational researchers? Do we use our emotional responses as the impetus for constructing new stories to live by? Is there something in our observations about teachers' knowledge, teachers' identities, and teachers' professional knowledge landscapes worthy of study?

Reflecting on his forty years of anthropological study of two provincial towns, Pare, Indonesia and Sefrow, Morocco, Geertz (1995) said of his visits to those towns, "It always seemed not the right time, but a pause between right times, between a turbulence somehow got through and another one obscurely looming" (p. 4). It never seemed like quite the right time for his studies. On sabbaticals, we feel, as Geertz says, as if we are in a pause, a resting place between happenings. We shall try, perhaps as Geertz did in his pauses, and as he does now in his 40-year retrospective, to make a little sense of what we see and feel.

Perhaps the most common way of making sense of the turbulence we observe is that it is a turbulence we will get through. Things will readjust and return to normal. Budget cuts are hurting, programs are being modified but, still, we persist and will ourselves to go on. Class sizes are larger; relations with administrators and parents are more fractious; students, sensing the turmoil, are more uproarious. But, we wait out the turbulence, sensing that the system will adjust and we with it: that we will come out of it, changed, yet the same in the most important ways, ways that define who we are, what we do, and why, ways that retain our professional identity.

But there is also the unease, not clearly articulated, dimly understood, that things will never be the same, that we will have to become new people, professionals with a different identity on a changed landscape. Professionals, professors and teachers, we sense, will need a new story to live by. Among the professors experiencing the most intense unease are those who have been the longest in the profession, closest to formal retirement, who opt with surprising and even shocking readiness to early retirement and buy-out packages. A recent *Globe and Mail* news story (Krueger, 1995), based on Renner's (1995) book on trends in higher education, pointed out that university professors, mostly hired during the postwar baby boom expansion, are now disillusioned with their professional lives. They had imagined an intellectual world filled with seminars, debates, and a high-minded teaching life. They now find themselves uncertain about who they are in environments where they are doing things undreamed of in their graduate studies days. The news story went on to say that with proper early-retirement packages, universities—and thereby their public government benefactors—could help solve their financial problems by offering people an alternative to a life no longer lived as when hired, certainly not as imagined in their graduate-studies youth.

The University of Alberta recently sent out a letter offering early retirement bonuses to 700 faculty members over age 50 with 10 years of university experience. Unprecedented numbers accepted the package in the faculty of education: over 40 faculty members out of a faculty complement of 116. The package was not that good—good, yes, but over a third of the faculty? Why? Anticipated lives and lived lives far apart; incommensurate professional landscapes.

So who are we on sabbatical? We have a sense of a changing world and we experience this with a sense of uncertainty, a sense shared by many of our colleagues and, undoubtedly, by many school teachers. Still, with Geertz, we are hesitant to trust this sense knowing that we are in the midst of something happening. We know that the landscape is changing. But we resonate with Geertz's words that "change, apparently, is not a parade that can be watched as it passes" (1995, p. 4). At first, we tried to imagine ourselves on sabbatical watching the metaphorical parade. But we know too well that we are in that parade. We know that our observations, our theoretical reflections on what is actually happening, and how we interpret and provide meaningful context to what is happening, cannot easily be trusted. What can be done? Geertz, trying to explain his two provincial towns, writes:

> You could contrast then and now, before and after, describe what life used to be like, what it has since become. You could write a narrative, a story of how one thing led to another, and those to a third: and then . . . You could invent indexes and describe trends: more individualism, less religiosity, rising welfare, declining morale. You could produce a memoir, look back at the past through the blaze of the present, struggling to re-experience. You could outline stages—Traditional, Modern, Postmodern; Feudalism, Colonialism, Independence—and postulate a goal for it all: the withered state, the iron cage. You could describe the transformation of institutions, structures in motion: the family, the market, the civil service, the school. You could even build a model, conceive a process, propose a theory. You could draw graphs. (1995, p. 1)

And so could we. We could do all of those things but, says Geertz, "it is not history one is faced with, nor biography, but a confusion of histories, a swarm of biographies. There is order in it all of some sort, but it is the order of the squall or a street market, nothing metrical" (p. 2).

A History, a Biography: Norman Beach on the English as a Second Language (ESL) Adult Education Landscape

Norman Beach teaches English as a second language to adults as part of a school board's continuing education program. The following excerpt (Phillion, 1995) describes one of his classes from a researcher's, Phillion's, point of view. Like most instructors with continuing education contracts, Norman has little tenure. His contract specifies a minimum of 10 students per class. His classes may meet in any available school board space. Norman himself is a certified teacher, but certification is not required for teaching adult ESL classes. As the excerpt begins Phillion arrives at school several minutes early with her colleague, Ming Fang He, and they mingle with students in the hall prior to class opening.

> At 9:25, we can enter the elementary classroom. From looking at the room, I can't see anything to indicate that adult ESL learners use it. The adult students file in and sit at small desks in rows facing the teacher and a chalk board. A sign on the board says "Please clean this room after use." Norman leaves to get a TV and video to show the last 15 minutes of "Forrest Gump." I wonder how this fits with the new City Board Curriculum Guidelines. According to these guidelines, Norman's lesson plans are to be based on student needs.
>
> After watching "Forrest Gump," Norman asks the students what they think the movie is really telling them. Some say they think it is saying that you have to look at more than someone's intelligence, you have to look at what is in their hearts. Norman weaves grammar, vocabulary, and pronunciation practice into the conversation. The talk shifts to why the girl in the movie died; AIDS and drug use are discussed. I realize that these classes are places for students to discuss important issues facing Canadian society. Norman meets the students' needs and fulfills the Curriculum Guidelines in many creative ways.
>
> At the break, students have coffee and jasmine tea. They contribute money each month. One woman brought Chinese pancakes she made this morning for a school breakfast program where she is employed. She gets up to go to work while her children are still sleeping. Ming Fang and some female students talk about fashion.
>
> After the break, we get into groups. My group has four women and one man. Three of the women are Chinese, one is from Burma and two from Hong Kong. The other woman is from Egypt, and the man is from Iraq. This group is reflective of how multicultural this, and other, Adult ESL classes are. Other students in the class are from Taiwan, mainland China, Vietnam, Morocco, Turkey, and Sri Lanka. They range in age from early twenties to late sixties. Some have been in Canada only a few months; one man has been here for forty years.
>
> We talk about our children. One woman has an eleven-month-old daughter. She leaves her in daycare so she can attend this class. She said her daughter learns so much there. Yesterday she came home and began to clap. She had never done this before. Another woman is congratulated on having four sons.

The students read a short newspaper story written by an immigrant from Chile. They have no trouble understanding the words "military dictatorship." The woman from Burma said this is what they have in her country. She says that the Chilean refugee in the story was lucky to come to Canada with a hundred dollars and two suitcases. She came with one suitcase, fifty dollars, and one gold ring. When she first came to Canada fifteen years ago, she could not study English. She was busy raising her children and taking care of her mother-in-law who was paralyzed.

Some of the students have to leave the class at eleven. The class hours have recently shifted and the new ones do not fit with their schedules. One man is going to pick up his grandchildren from school. A few others leave for work.

In another paper about Norman, He (1995) describes him as the only child in a dentist's family. She writes:

Norman was not very interested in education until he got a Bachelor of Arts in History at Carleton University. He was fascinated by progressive education in the early seventies. Along with his idealistic ideas about education, he dropped his original dream of being a writer, and went to a teachers' college. He found it difficult to teach a high school class because he quickly got angry at the students. He became discouraged, returned to his original plans of becoming a writer, and began work in a publishing company. Because of his interests in politics, he went to South America and worked as a language teacher. Drawing on university ESL courses and his classroom teaching, he began to develop his own teaching ideas and techniques. Eventually, he returned to Toronto where he started teaching adults.

The next excerpt is a series of Norman's reflections on his teaching (He, 1995).

I see myself as not only an instructor, but also as a sort of intermediary or liaison person between English Canadian society and the learners. Obviously, I am not a sociological expert who can explain everything and solve all problems, but often I am the first English Canadian a learner gets to know. When they leave the class, some learners refer to this in cards or letters to me. So I feel a bit like a "welcoming ambassador" for English Canada. . . . I try to make the classroom as happy, fun-loving and warm an environment as possible, and I tell a lot of anecdotes about my family and friends, so that the learners have a personal connection with me. That's why I brought my mother and father in to meet the learners. Of course, I'm not saying that everybody should do this, but I enjoy it. The learners do too.

The other reason I see part of my job as being a social facilitator is that people communicate best with those they feel comfortable with. So I do what I can to help change the classroom from a collection of strangers into a community of friends. . . . So this is what I see myself as: a language instructor, a liaison person, and a social facilitator. . . . There are routine elements of this job, so if you focused on teaching the material, you could get bored. Very occasionally, particularly in the afternoon when I'm copying, when I photocopy a handout I've used since before the Flood, I might have to suppress a yawn. But that's when you have to remember that—you're not teaching material, you are teaching people. And to do a good job, you have to be aware of their needs and their progress. That's a very tall order.

In these excerpts, we see a teacher. Though Norman is teaching what many would consider to be nontraditional classes made up of diverse age groups, with people at different stages in their life cycles and from all over the world, these excerpts reveal a person clearly identifiable as a teacher. An elementary school teacher of 6-year-old children would recognize Norman, teacher of students into their 60s, as a member of the profession, or, at least, as a person who shared a teaching identity.

Norman works to plan his curriculum around student needs. In doing this he responds, in part, to board of education guidelines. He works to establish a community in his classroom: He sets up small groups, shares his personal life with his students and encourages them to share theirs, brings his parents to class, shows films, and is flexible in allowing his adult students to meet their diverse commitments. In sum, Norman lives a teacher's life in the classroom.

At one level, we are surprised that a teacher of such dramatically different students from those ordinarily thought to comprise public school education, and who teaches in the continuing education program, not part of the regular board program and, therefore, not part of the Board-Teacher Federation contract negotiations, is so recognizable as a teacher. But Norman not only identifies himself as a teacher, he is identifiable as such. Upon observing Norman, one confidently says, "There is a teacher."

But close up, if we try to understand Norman's identity on education's changing professional knowledge landscape, what do we see? We are, looking closely at his professional knowledge landscape, bemused by the easy identification of Norman as a teacher. To think of Norman and his land-scape in the context of the larger educational landscape, the one that we sense as uncertain, leads us to wonder how he continues to go about his teaching at all, let alone with, it appears, an unruffled teacher identity. Even though he is clearly caught up in Geertz's passing parade, the story Norman lives by seems unchanging. As we search for the "order of the squall or the streetmarket" on education's changing professional knowledge landscape, we look for signs of a new story to live by.

A Sequence of Stories to Live by
on the Professional Knowledge Landscape

Like Geertz and his 40 years in the field, we may identify ourselves . . . we may give ourselves identity . . . by telling a story of a changing landscape in terms of a series of stages. One of us tells his story as being hired at the tail end of the huge expansion in secondary and postsecondary education that occurred in the 1960s.

> I came to the Ontario Institute for Studies in Education at a time
> when doctoral graduates in North America had opportunities to enter
> university teaching almost anywhere they chose on the continent. We
> were given inducements, courted, and, in my own case, hired and
> given a year at Chicago to complete my dissertation before taking up
> my work in Toronto. I arrived in Toronto in the summer of 1968 to
> find myself sharing, with another recent hiree from Chicago, still a
> 1996 colleague, a research officer, and a secretary, no questions
> asked, no grant forms to complete. In addition, there were few limits
> on conference travel. Research funds were available for the most
> minimal idea. My colleagues and I frequently refer to ourselves as the
> lucky ones, having, as we see it, got in just under the wire. My first
> year or so, novice though I was to the ways of academe, were spent
> on search committees, far-flung phone calls to track people down,
> and too many heavy faculty recruitment lunches. That stopped.
> Before the next decade was over my colleagues and I agonized in
> committee meetings over the ethics of admitting doctoral students to
> programs where the opportunities for graduate employment were nil,
> or so we now tell the story.

Others will tell the story slightly differently, the timing will be off a year or two here or there, things in Canada somewhat different from in the United States, the British and Australian scenes different again, and so forth. Though these details are hazy, the plotline of the story hirees of the late 1960s tell is pretty much the same.

As we wrote this paper we momentarily came to a difficult spot because, it turned out, both of us were essentially telling the same story—"I had it good and my students have it bad"—though one of us took his first job in 1968 and the other took hers in 1984. Landscape stories that should have been different were the same.

I told a story of graduating in 1983, of finding, after many applications, a university position, and an opportunity to build new programs. I moved to my current position where I created a research and development center. "Who can do that now?" I wondered. "Certainly not my students!" I told stories of my graduate students who are now struggling to find tenure-stream positions, and who often take term-contract positions where the positions are defined entirely in terms of teaching and supervision duties. These are students who would have been top university prospects, the kind of people, with academic credentials, that would have been first in line in either 1968 or 1983.

We do not know how graduates of the 1990s will tell their stories; we can only imagine them to be ones of some desperation, of feelings of being lost as the parade moves along. What sense do we make of this?

Less, we think, than is commonly thought to be possible. We could, as in the outline for Geertz's hypothetical narrative, tell "a story of how one thing led to another, and those to a third: 'and then . . . and then.'" Following Geertz's lead, we could name three stages to fit our stories since 1968, Expansion and Hallelujah (1968), Belt Tightening and Stabilization (1984), Reduction, Cutbacks, and Downsizing (1996). We might argue about these dates. The British would see it somewhat differently and tell us that the labels were not quite right and the dates were off by at least a decade; and the Americans would tell us that the story is too simple, has many more ups and downs with governing parties, and especially, presidents—Kennedy, Johnson, Nixon, Ford, Reagan, Clinton. But our account would be arguable and that means somewhat credible, a plausible explanation. And so we would have a degree of intellectual comfort in knowing where we had been, where we are now, and where we are going, an overall story of the passing parade.

We do not think so. Partly we are in events, a parade, and thereby unable to understand it and our part in it as we march along. This is not a military parade: It is one of semichaos with movements here and there and no one marching in unison. Nevertheless, the parade moves on, and to where?

It is that "to where" that is so puzzling, so burdened with potential in our scramble for maintaining, and creating, a new sense of identity on this landscape. Nobody said, in 1968, as they do with the Toronto Santa Claus Parade, that it begins at Bathurst and Bloor and ends at Queen's Park. We are just in the parade hurrying along and no one has said where it ends and no one knows the route that it is taking.

The 1995 Nobel Prize for Economics was recently given to Robert E. Lucas for an economic theory relevant to our discussion. Lucas found that, in part, economic futures are so unpredictable (one of the facts of economics) and, therefore, so unmanageable (a related fact), because economic models assume that people do not think; that people do not adjust their spending decisions and other behavior in response to their fears and expectations about their futures. The models assume that people will continue to act without adjusting their behavior as if the trends at any one time, the direction our metaphorical parade seems to be going, will continue into the future. The factors and forces, the so-called theoretical constructs that seem to be at work with the last downturn, upturn, or shift in economic direction, are manipulated to project a nuanced view of the economic future. But the predictions do not work, because they assume that the noticeable direction and the noticeable forces and factors correlated with shifts in direction are the only things that move the parade. In our terms what Lucas points out is that people and what they may decide to think also move the parade. The direction of the metaphorical economic parade is impossible to predict.

So, where is our parade, our professional knowledge landscape, headed? Many pretend to know: "It is all downhill," "It will straighten out when things return to normal, once we are over the hurdle," and so forth. Maybe, maybe not. It depends, partly, on what people think.

And who are those people and what do they think? The first is easier to suggest an answer for than is the second. The first is everybody. It is not only the people in the parade, it is the people watching the parade, it is the parade organizers, it is the people indifferent to the parade. What happens on the university landscape is part of what happens in society more generally and this, in turn, is part of what is happening in the world. As Geertz remarked in his anthropologist's tour of 4 decades, "The problem is that more has changed, and more disjointedly, than one at first imagines." Geertz goes on to point out that it is not only, for him, the towns studied and the countries within which the towns reside, but also world politics, the relationship of these countries to the world and, indeed, the discipline, anthropology in his case, for studying these towns, even, the anthropologist, Geertz, himself, that have changed. The same is true for the university landscape. Both of us look at the landscape from a 1996 vantage point. One thinks he knows something about 1968, 1984, and 1996, but what? The other thinks she knows something about 1984 and 1996, but what? Everything, including these two observers, has changed since 1968. We need to understand something about it all.

Norman's Stories to Live by on the Adult ESL Professional Knowledge Landscape

Leaving Norman, we felt bemused that he was so easily identifiable as a teacher. We did not share our reasons for this surprise but by now readers will doubtless have a sense of our thinking. Here it is in brief. Norman identifies himself as, and is identifiable as, a teacher. He does the sorts of things that good teachers do. Yet he works on a landscape almost unrecognizable as a teacher's landscape, certainly not the kind of landscape he was prepared for in his teacher education studies, and most certainly not the landscape we observe in the passing parade from our sabbatical vantage points.

Teachers, for the most part, work in schools, with in- and out-of-classroom places. So does Norman. But Norman's in-classroom place is not easily recognizable as his in the sense that teachers often claim a classroom as "mine." As JoAnn walks into Norman's classroom she sees no sign that Norman had been there before, "nothing to indicate that adult ESL learners use it." And just in case Norman thinks to leave marks of his passing, a sign on the board that is clearly a message from the regular teacher to the adult ESL teacher says, "Please clean this room after use." In fact Norman's classroom space could, with little warning, be shifted to another location.

Not only Norman's classroom space but also his class size is a shifting matter. Salima, a Moroccan immigrant from Casablanca whom JoAnn befriends in Norman's class, "feels guilty that she cannot come to class every day because she has to work. She knows that Norman has to have 10 students to keep the class open." Norman is paid on an hourly basis and only if classes remain, on average, above the minimal figure. Ming Fang He, a part-time adult ESL teacher like Norman, writes:

Most of the ESL teachers can only work on a part-time basis. In order to survive, they have to have second or third occupations. Our salary is hourly paid and our lesson planning time is not paid. Most of us have had some sort of exposure to a second culture and language. Our knowledge base has to touch upon a variety of resources on Canadian culture, history, government, etc. in order to facilitate our students' participation fully in Canadian society. Every day we rush to and from our different occupations. Our classes could be closed any day if the student quota is reduced. Physically, our classroom spaces are located at every possible space the public schools could offer after their own purposes are met for the public school students. Our classrooms are squeezed into formal institutions, community agencies, libraries, and apartment buildings for easy access by the learner.

JoAnn Phillion, on another occasion, writes,

Nothing prepared me for some of the City Board adult ESL sites that I visited. Many of these sites are isolated, teachers and students are on their own except for monthly visits from lead instructors. . . . I vividly recall one site located in an old apartment building that smelled of toilets and the attempts to mask those odors. The classroom was cramped, students sat on old folding chairs, the grey paint peeled from the walls, the grey linoleum peeled from the floor.

Ming Fang He points out that class size changes from day to day because of several factors: People are there on a volunteer basis; those who work tend to be in positions of low job stability; some work "on call"; many reside in an area for only short periods of time.

It may appear that Norman has only the barest of an in-classroom place on the landscape and no out-of-classroom place. But this would be a misreading of the situation. He does have an in-classroom place in exactly the same conceptual way that other teachers do. But it is a very different in-classroom place with, apparently, somewhat ad hoc location assignment arrangements and the requirement that the ESL classroom not leave traces from day to day. Still, strange as it may appear to a regular classroom teacher, Norman has an in-classroom place on his professional knowledge landscape. And here is part of the puzzle we sensed: How can Norman be so easily identifiable as a teacher when his in-classroom place on the landscape is so different from the in-classroom landscape for which he was educated and in which others teach?

Norman's out-of-classroom place is so dramatically different as to suggest that he has none. There is no staffroom, no cafeteria, no student-teacher library. There are two central adult ESL offices in disparate sections of the city and each have tiny resource libraries. There are a cadre of lead teachers, former teachers like Norman, promoted to positions of supervision and board accountability. Policies, programs, and new directives reach Norman via these people and are discussed in associations like, yet not like, teacher unions. Norman has nowhere near the degree of union-sponsored professional protection that regular teachers employed by the board enjoy. Still, Norman is identifiable as a teacher. And if his in-classroom place on the landscape seems different and odd by comparison with the in-classroom place ordinarily associated with regular teachers, Norman's out-of-classroom place is barely recognizable as part of a teacher's professional knowledge landscape.

These matters alone are puzzling when we think of Norman's identity as a teacher. In what is undoubtedly an immense oversimplification, we might imagine that Norman's teacher identity was formed as a student with teachers; subsequently shaped by his teacher education program; and fine-tuned by virtue of proximity to teachers in the regular school system, so close, but yet so far, from Norman's own in- and out-of-classroom places on the landscape. Norman is a teacher. He thinks of himself as a teacher: he is identifiable as a teacher. And he knows that, being on the margins of the formal school system, his professional world, his professional knowledge landscape, is most at risk. It is a puzzle, in fact a double puzzle: Why is Norman so easily identifiable as a teacher on his very different adult ESL in-classroom place on the landscape when times are good, or at least not bad, and how does this identity hold while the out-of-classroom place on the landscape shifts and changes with the passing parade?

What sense do we make of this? Again, less than is commonly thought to be possible. Again, following Geertz's lead, we could outline a narrative or series of stages. Adult ESL education, like special education and early childhood education, are on the margins of the school system. They were the last to become attached to board functions and are one of the first to go. We could, watching this passing parade, write an adult ESL education history, like that of Geertz's 40 years in anthropology, or that of our 1968 to 1996 changing university landscape. In Canada, that history would be tied to expansionist immigration policies, the financial wealth and social justice energy of the expansion period noted earlier, and the downloading from federal to provincial and local jurisdictions of language and labor service training and education. The movements in the 1996 ESL parade put everything familiar in question. Indeed, even the immigration policy engine is shifting with new proposed policies requiring English speaking capabilities as a Canadian immigration criterion.

Making Sense of Uncertainty

What are we doing as we view the education profession from a sabbatical resting place in the rhythm of activity and solitude of academic life? Is there an inquiry as we make our observations, feel uncertain about our responses, and put our thoughts on paper? Can somebody in a parade feel something about its passing and remark on it in ways that leave indelible traces; indelible meaning only that something sufficiently interesting is said to capture another's interest and help explain, for a time, an aspect of passing events? Asking the question is also more than solipsistic soul searching, or so we wish to think. It is a legitimate question that we social scientists need to carry with us as we both go about our inquiries and the educating of others into our habits, and as we rethink our identity as inquirers and teachers on the landscape. If, so central to our 1968 and 1984 professors' identities, the promise that educational research will better educate in noticeable and public ways is vastly overblown, as we now believe it to be, then our new identity must take hold óf a much more modest sense of our impact on the parade's direction. We need to stop worrying so much about educational change and development, school improvement, and processes of ensuring reform. But if our identity as the grand thinkers, understanders, and interpreters of the passing educational landscape needs sharp redefinition, it does not, we think, mean that we need to give up entirely. There is still, as Geertz remarked of his field and his working landscape, "order in it all of some sort," something that

> calls thus not for plotted narrative, measurement, reminiscence, or structural progression, and certainly not for graphs; though these have their uses . . . it calls for showing how particular events and unique occasions, an encounter here, a development there, can be woven together with a variety of facts and a battery of interpretations to produce a sense of how things go, have been going, and are likely to go. (p. 3)

And this is why our question is not mere solipsism. It is possible to take on an identity, composed partially of a research methodology with humble hopes, that may fit us as members of the passing parade. But we believe that we need to stop acting as if we knew so much, stop acting quite so knowingly and morally as social commentators on equity, social justice, and so on; and more to the point of this paper, stop educating teachers, teacher educators, and our own doctoral student replacements as if the landscape will return to normal and everything will be all right, although perhaps modified and downsized.

We do not know what this new identity might entail. A metaphor of Bateson's (1994) might be a helpful guide. She explained that large buildings are no longer built on rock-solid foundations but, rather, are built to float, like ocean liners. We need somehow to think of our research, our education of teachers, teacher educators, and doctoral replacements as building on a shifting, floating foundation.

Let us for a moment return to Norman yet again. What, to us, is the relevance of juxtaposing Norman's story with our own? Here is how we explain it. We are concerned with the changing professional knowledge landscape of education. We, and Norman, are teachers on the same landscape, at least the same general landscape, members of the same overall parade although not stepping side by side. We are in privileged settings, quite able to tell ourselves, in fact, that nothing need change. Academic life is getting tougher. We may need to take on a few extra students in courses that are somewhat less exciting than those driven entirely by our research, but, mostly, we will get by. We can continue to teach teachers for the schools as if the schools were not changing, and leave it up to the profession to juggle and adjust the identities of their members without assistance on our part; and we can continue to educate doctoral students into lives like our own, encouraging them to get line items for their résumés, participate in every bit of research they can while doctoral students, and negotiate hard with potential employers about the right to teach graduate courses, limit preservice supervision, codefine a reasonable teaching load. We can do that. We can proceed with a mostly unruffled identity. Norman, although he appears equally unruffled, cannot. If we can act as if our landscape were only losing a little of its green spring luster as the rains recede and the sun gets hotter, Norman must act as if his landscape were about to take on a shape no one really imagines, not the teachers on it and not the planners of it who have uncertain, but certainly less by a large margin, resources. Norman, knowing full well something of Bateson's shifting foundations, plans to leave Canada for teaching abroad. Is this a creative identity response to a shifting landscape? Or is it a somewhat desperate attempt to hold onto an existing identity? Perhaps, indeed, surely a bit of both.

Stories to Live by on the Shifting Landscape

Sue McKenzie-Robblee, a principal in one of the schools in the University of Alberta Faculty of Education's alternative teacher education program, recently commented that the regular teacher education program was so disconnected from schools as to be mostly pointless. She said that students needed to be in the schools, in the communities, and in other out-of-classroom places where teachers carry out their work. She said that the faculty's heavy emphasis on how to be a good teacher—meaning, how to be good with children in a classroom—was out of touch. If what we observe about the educational landscape is at all relevant, then McKenzie-Robblee's comments make a great deal of sense. Behind them is the implication that the university and its professors of teacher education are out of touch: Their identities as teacher educators and their imagined identities for teachers no longer work as useful guides for preparing teachers for the schools. Whereas the professors can continue to live their professors' stories, the teachers they teach, says McKenzie-Robblee, can no longer live by the stories of teaching offered by their professors. Professors' stories to live by can, although inappropriate to the landscape, continue. Teachers' stories to live by cannot. We see this in Norman's story. The professors' imagined stories of the teachers' stories to live by, which they teach to their students, are inappropriate to the changing professional knowledge landscape.

In our last book (Clandinin & Connelly, 1995), we told Marion Connelly's story. To recap, Marion began teaching in a one-room rural Grades 1–9 Alberta school in the 1920s. Her career, if it could be called that in those days, spanned 40 years, interrupted from time to time by babies and Marion's sense of their needs. Lee School was Marion's only school until it closed in the 1950s and she was transferred to Lundbreck School, a centralized Grades 1–12 school, replete with a principal, classrooms for each grade, and a sports program. For Marion, the move was a major adjustment in her professional knowledge landscape. Never again could she hold the teacher identity developed over her 20 years in Lee School.

We gave a partial rendition of this in our earlier account of Marion's life. Our interest there was to focus on the shifting relations of in-classroom, out-of-classroom, and personal landscape matrix features in Marion's life. We showed that the moral authority for her sense of identity as a teacher was given in very different ways in Lee School from in Lundbreck School, with a supervising principal, a supervisory official with whom she did not have a personal relationship, and the loss of a sense of professional ownership: a loss as Marion moved into the larger professional knowledge community and a loss as her husband relinquished his role as the sole school trustee. Our 1968 and 1984 professors' professional knowledge landscapes are, of course, direct heirs to Marion's changing landscape; so too is our 1996 professors' professional knowledge landscape; heir, too, is Norman's professional knowledge landscape, part of the same parade that passed through southern Alberta.

As they say, too late wise. What, we would like to ask Marion, did she think of her story of herself as a teacher as her landscape shifted? Did she feel uncertain about how to continue to work as a teacher? Did she wonder who she was, a person who had heretofore been given an identity by virtue of a certain kind of educational world? We imagine that she may well have said some of the same things that we now say in this paper. "Things," she might have said, "are in a state of transition, flux, even, it seems, radical change." She might have felt nostalgic, lost, or frightened by what she observed and what it meant for her, or she may have been excited, seeing new possibilities and opportunities for her teacher story to live by. Certainly, for her, much would be different in her professional life. She would never know her students in the same way, students who were children of neighboring ranching families, most of whom knew one another more closely than most neighbors in downtown

Toronto apartment buildings. At Lundbreck School, Marion had children with families she only distantly knew, if at all, mixed in with others who came with her from Lee School. Her role in the community shifted dramatically. School concerts, sports programs, and other events tied Lee School intimately to its community and Marion to both. Douglas Connelly, rancher and keeper of family memories, goes over the old school records from time to time talking about the families, what has happened to their generations of children, who. owns their land, their deeds and misdeeds. But the parade continues indifferent to, but intimately connected with, Lee School records.

The changing professional knowledge landscape in those days, no different than the landscape of today, is embedded in, part of, the world around it. Part influenced by the world, part influencing it, the foundations of education shift. When Marion began teaching in southern Alberta, her home, and Lee School, had outdoor toilets, no refrigeration, no electricity, no telephones, few of the amenities we take for granted. There were trails for roads. During the summer months, milk was kept in a bucket in Connelly Creek to keep it cool. Rural electrification, telephone, highways and cars, indoor toilets and showers were welcome additions to Marion's life. And these additions were part and parcel of the shifting professional knowledge landscape. They were the very things, at least some of the very things, that resulted in the closing of Lee School and Marion's move to Lundbreck School.

The landscape, not merely the metaphor to which we refer, but the physical landscape, the ownership boundaries, were shifting dramatically in Marion's time.

> As a boy I became a stacker in haying season. Hay, cattle feed, was swept across the hay fields with a team of horses to an overshot stacker where another team of horses activated the overshot to throw the hay onto a stack. The stacker sorted it out and built a weather resistant top. My younger brother never learned to stack. The three year age difference between us coincided with a mechanization of the ranching operation and stacking of loose hay became obsolete. Winter cattle feeding and water hole opening was a full-time job for my father and his help; today my brother does both in an hour or so mostly from the comfort of a heated truck cab. These changes in our ranch were mirrored throughout rural Alberta and were part and parcel of Marion's transition from Lee School to Lundbreck School. Increased mechanization and communication resulted in a sharp decrease in the rural population. Most left the ranches. Those that remained bought up the land, my brother responsible for his share of this depopulating of the landscape. Rural children vanished. So did their one-room schools, and so did their teachers.

Those who chart the trends and plot the graphs, would, surely, have projected mega-ranching operations based on the Alberta trends. But these imagined scientific projections would not, on close inspection, even appear to hold in general. It is well known, for example, that large agricultural conglomerates in the United States have encountered serious economic inefficiencies that come down to people making a difference to the projected trends, a reminder of the Nobel laureate, Lucas, noted above. Smaller ranchers and farmers, using smaller equipment, use the land in and around bogs, swamps, lakes, trees, the nooks of tillable land. Larger, more efficient machinery can only handle, with ease, large rectangularly laid out plots of land. The rest falls into disuse. Furthermore, the smaller operator tinkers with the equipment. In Marion's time, tinkerers were referred to as "barbed-wire Johnnies," people who could keep their equipment running with a little fencing wire. The large operators, the agribusinesses, buy new equipment or work on an equipment-lease basis. Repair costs are low, capital costs proportionally higher. These sorts of matters have influenced Marion's Alberta community but so has another phenomenon, one that planners would have been unable to predict at the time. The Lee School area, given modern transportation, is now seen as not too far away from major urban centers and, because it is considered to be a beautiful physical landscape, located as it is in the foothills of the Rocky Mountains, is in demand for recreational use. The population is again increasing and land prices have escalated. People are confounding the trends.

What can we make of Marion's shifting landscape? Less, perhaps, than some who are bitter about the loss of the good old days and less than those who think that through research and an understanding of the landscape they can stop or redirect the changes: more, perhaps, in the sense of contextualizing education's professional knowledge parade and seeing it both as effect and cause, an influential, and influenced, particle in a changing world. For the simple, homespun contextualizing of Marion's landscape above, we see that her shifting professional knowledge landscape was part of a shifting rural community and this, again, as part of changes, a parade of changes, in every social niche. Few things could, from a 1996 perspective, be said to be staying the same. Marion's parade is the same parade that we see from our sabbatical vantage points.

We believe that there are lessons in this for our stories to live by as researchers as we observe our changing professional knowledge landscape, try to understand it, and consider what, if anything, we might do to dress up the parade in some small way. After all, parades can be made colourful and interesting by virtue of the habits of parade members. This, it seems, is the role of research and teaching at universities—parade participants but rarely parade organizers. The researcher identity as a parade organizer was strongly evident in the late 1960s and 1970s. Even now signs of such a researcher identity are detected in research efforts to reform teacher education, return schools to parents, restructure education, foster school-based curriculum development, account for public support in terms of student achievement. Some might think that metaphorically positioning educational researchers as parade participants relative to the professional world is not enough. For some, it may very well not be. There is little glitter and grandeur in our notion of how the profession, at any level, may take hold of its destiny. Researchers cannot, we believe, organize the parade; they cannot know where it is going; they cannot tell it where to go. But in our view, this is all we have ever had, notwithstanding academic chutzpah on the potential and power of educational research, notwithstanding the ambitions and political impact of teachers' organizations, and notwithstanding the recent efforts to increase professional self-governance and the specification of pedagogical and content knowledge seen as the route to a new enhanced professional status.

Researchers can, we believe, dress up the parade in some small way as they participate in it. For us, this is where the hope, the sense of possibility, lies. In working through the ideas in this paper, we have come to see that the changing landscape and teachers' and researchers' professional identities, their stories to live by, are interconnected. Just as the parade changes everything— the things, the people, the relationships, the parade itself—as it passes, so, too, do teachers' and researchers' identities need to change. It is not so much that teachers and researchers, professionals on the landscape, need new identities, new stories to live by: they need shifting, changing identities; shifting, changing stories to live by as the parade offers up new possibilities and cancels out others. The professional knowledge landscape does not stand still. It is not fixed—not in Marion's time, not in our time, not in the future. Likewise, professional identities are not fixed. For we researchers and teacher educators, our place in the parade is not, therefore, to educate for a fixed landscape and for a fixed identity but, rather, to educate for shifting stories to live by.

Dancing in the Passing Parade

Returning to where we began this paper, we noted an unease, not clearly articulated, dimly understood, that things will never be the same, that we will have to become new people, professionals with a different identity on a changed landscape. There is talk of schools and universities disappearing, at least as they currently exist. For example, one parade trend projects, on the basis of what is now known about teaching and the imagined potential of technology, that students and teachers may rarely if ever meet, except perhaps via an electronic link. A student who lives in Egypt plans to do an Ontario Institute for Studies in Education master's degree entirely by E-mail. Whereas this is virtually unheard of in this institution, it is already common-place in others. Playing out this parade trend, without consideration of the interaction of the people in the parade, reminded us of ghost towns, and we imagined the possibility of ghost schools and ghost universities, physical relics of a landscape through which the parade has passed. We thought again of Marion's landscape, long past the ghost-school phase. Marion's ranch is home to two one-room schools, one now a horse barn/tack room and the other a museum piece. These were the lucky schools. Firgrove School, for example, not far from Lee, is nothing more than a spot on a hay meadow that the rancher who now owns the land points out while driving.

It is not as if the profession of education has not witnessed changes as far reaching and dramatic as those we now observe: It just seems that way because of the time span—people joining a parade, marching, dancing along, and leaving before something as visibly dramatic as the ghost school shows up. But, as Marion's story shows, schools such as Lee that were in many respects more integrally related to community life, more central to its social fabric than are most modern-day schools, disappeared entirely from the land-scape. The disappearance of schools as we know them in 1996, though trou-bling for most to anticipate, may well be part of the passing parade. If so, what will take their place? In Marion's day it was schools such as Lundbreck, schools that our grandfathers and grandmothers could hardly imagine. As it was, at the time that Lee School became a ghost school, a host of related parade trends occurred, modifying, in mostly positive ways, the quality of Marion's overall life, not only her identity as a teacher. And so it will be for us, for Norman, for other teachers, we imagine, with the passing of univer-sities and schools, should that happen, in 1996 and beyond.

PART III

Administrator Stories, Stories of Administrators, System Stories

In Part III we shift from teachers and schools to administrators in their schools and in their systems. As we listened to teachers' and administrators' stories and thought about how they were positioned on the landscape, we realized that there were differences between administrators' stories and teachers' stories that influenced the relationship between knowledge, content, and identity. Our understanding of these differences led us to separate these stories from those in Part I, although we realized that administrators may have strong teacher identities. In Part III there are three administrator stories. We are very much aware that not only in this book but in previous work we have paid more attention to classroom teachers and to their stories. When we reflect on the stories of Part I all of this prior work shapes our thinking. The three stories in Part III are only a beginning in trying to hear and understand administrator knowledge, context, and identity.

CHAPTER 12

A First-Year Vice-Principal's Position on the Landscape: In- and Out-of-Classroom Splits

Florence Samson

During my years of trying to integrate personal and professional life I have experienced splits, tensions, and dilemmas, as I attempted to merge my ideals and realities. Reflecting on my first year in administration, I found that conflicting loyalties (Bateson, 1994) existed not only between the personal and professional spheres of my life, but also within the professional spheres. As teaching administrator, I experienced similar splits, tensions, and dilemmas within my professional life as I went about my daily tasks at school.

Teacher/Administrator: Split Roles, Split Loyalties

I had been working on my doctorate in a province distant from my own. Previous to that I had been a teacher. I returned home to take up a vice-principal's position, one in which the school enrollment of almost 600 children dictated that I be half-time teacher and half-time vice-principal. When the previous female principal had retired at the end of the school year, the staff wanted the then male vice-principal, with whom they enjoyed excellent rapport, to replace her. Despite spoken and written protests, the board appointed someone else. The principal, Robert, seven teachers, and I were newly appointed to our staff of 34. I came into this situation as a novice vice-principal. One of my earliest stories of working in this situation is that of the first staff meeting.

I anticipated this meeting with great trepidation. What might happen? The agenda had been well planned by the principal and me, but we did not know what to expect. The meeting was to be held in the Library/Resource Center where four or five people could be seated at each of the round tables. To ensure mingling, I scotch-taped a variety of poems and illustrations to the tables and cut duplicates into puzzle pieces, which I gave to staff members as they entered, explaining that the finding of the matching pieces would determine seating. Everyone complied with my request and I felt that the meeting began on a pleasant note. Shortly after it started, Robert was called to the telephone. I found myself filling in for him.

> Some teachers look at their watches, flip through their folders, and glance furtively at each other. I wish I could get through this agenda. . . . Is there anything that I can skip? . . . Item 25 . . . Teachers have more important things to do—their supplies are not put away, their classrooms are not ready. . . . So much to be done. So little time . . . Item 35 . . . Should I allow any more discussion on this particular topic? No, it can wait until next week's meeting! Item 54 . . . My adrenalin is flowing! . . . The end is in sight. . . . Do the teachers feel my tension?
>
> The meeting ends. I understand their sighs of relief—at my last staff meeting, I was teacher, not administrator. As teachers move out, I say, "Thank you for your time! I know how difficult it was to sit through this meeting. Good luck with the preparations for tomorrow!"
>
> They are happy to retreat to their classrooms. . . . Are they ready to meet their students? . . . Have they absorbed all the messages passed down from the Department of Education, through the School Board, through Robert and me, to them? Did Robert and I fulfill our roles and pass the messages on in an appropriate and meaningful way?
>
> Even while Robert and I thank the teachers as they retreat to their classrooms, I dismiss any thought I have of my own preparedness to meet my students, for I will not begin my remedial reading teaching for several days. For the present, I am administrator.

For many teachers, already aware of expectations of both board and school, the meeting was probably boring. But for the newly appointed, the meeting and the printed contents of the folder provided information which would mark out the boundaries of what was expected and acceptable in our positions as employees of this particular board, and in this particular school. Later, when Robert and I reflected on the meeting, we felt happy. We had survived our first staff meeting, and I had completed my first official task as an administrator. But even as I chaired the staff meeting, about which I would later feel happy, I experienced the tensions created by being both teacher and administrator. These tensions would stay with me throughout my tenure in this position, for they were the consequences of the divided loyalties inherent in my split role.

Teacher/Administrator: Split Loyalties

As a teaching vice-principal, there were certain periods of the day when I taught small groups of primary students who were experiencing reading difficulties. When not in the classroom, I carried out administrative duties. There were times when I was pulled in different directions as both teaching and administration vied for my attention and time. Administrative duties often took priority over my teaching duties, but rarely was the reverse true. For example, in Robert's absence from the school premises during my teaching periods, at times when a substitute was not provided for him, discipline, sick children, and emergency situations took priority over teaching. Being taken from my teaching troubled me. My loyalties were split between administration and teaching. I had to make difficult choices between my responsibilities to colleagues and students. Moreover, I thought some teachers did not always understand why I canceled classes to deal with administrative tasks that demanded immediate attention. I felt the split physically, emotionally, and mentally. Whenever administrative duties demanded immediate attention, I was forced to neglect my teaching duties, and my responsibilities to both my students and teacher colleagues. When my remedial reading students were not taken out of the regular classrooms, teachers' plans were disrupted. I felt that they resented this. These situations created inner conflict for me. As a result, I found that I was continually trying to explain myself. I felt accountable to everyone—teachers, students, and Robert.

Teacher/Administrator: Divided Spaces—Classroom/Office

My feeling of split and unsettled existence, due to my split assignment, was heightened by the separation of the classroom and office spaces allocated to me. Neither my office, nor my classroom, was exclusively my territory. As a full-time teacher I had always had my own classroom. As teacher/administrator I did not. My vice-principal's office was used by everyone. It was the visitors' coat closet, storage area, meeting room, and telephone booth for private calls. I did not have a computer in my office and was forced to wait my turn for the secretary's, which was located in the general office. There I was constantly interrupted. I had no clearly defined administrative territory.

Just as troubling was my classroom space. It was the nurse's room, a 14-by-8-foot windowless area, shared by itinerant teachers and other professionals who came to teach or meet with students. Not only was this a shared space, but it was too small to allow me to teach in the way that I believed I should. I felt compromised in what I could do for and with the children. However, I claimed this territory more aggressively than I did my vice-principal's office. I covered the walls with evidence of the time that the children and I spent together. This connection with the children was my lifeline, my safe place on the landscape. It brought me back to my professional center, to the thread of common purpose that cemented my split role of teacher and administrator.

I felt the tension of living in two places. I found myself clinging to the safe classroom space. Living in the out-of-classroom space as an administrator was too exposed. It was not that I felt vulnerable in that space—afraid of the challenge. Rather it was that my agenda was never mine, but always someone else's. The out-of-classroom landscape brought me into the mainstream of life at the school. Here I was responsible for the complexity of the operation of the whole school, whereas within the classroom landscape I was responsible for what happened within my own room. Within our classroom students and I could adapt my agenda as needed. In the administrative position the agenda was rarely mine.

Teacher/Administrator: Split Times

My feelings of split existence were heightened by the demands made on my time by both administration and teaching responsibilities. Although neat boxes on my timetable suggested a definite division between administrative and teaching time, teaching time was frequently invaded by administrative tasks. These neat boxes suggested recess and lunch breaks each day. These rarely, if ever, occurred. Such times were filled with supervising children in the front foyer, answering the telephone, responding to emergencies, seeing parents, doing lunch duty, and running the office. The before- and after-school hours, blank spaces on my timetable, were also filled with administrative tasks.

Robert and I had an understanding that I would arrive at school before other staff to meet early-arriving children. Robert, the teachers, and secretary did not arrive until much later. My first 45 minutes at school were spent in the same way I spent recess and noon hours. When not attending after-school meetings, I responded to office demands. I felt that I was constantly in a reactive rather than proactive mode. There were no protected blocks of time in which to reflect on action. Reflection took place in action (Schön, 1983).

All of these administrative demands on the out-of-classroom landscape removed me from teaching and often prevented me from being proactive. They kept me from the curriculum planning and staff professional growth and development which had attracted me initially to the position. I enjoyed the time spent with my students, and felt a sense of accomplishment—a coming together—in working with them. But I also wanted to implement some of the teacher development practices that had been the focus of my doctoral studies. However, the moment I stepped outside the classroom—sometimes, even when I was still inside the classroom—I was seen as administrator, and constantly on call by teachers, custodial staff, school board personnel, students, parents, interns, substitutes, salespersons, delivery persons, maintenance staff, and anyone else who contacted the office. On the out-of-classroom place on the landscape these concerns took priority over my teaching and the boxes on my neat timetable.

Teacher/Administrator: Feeling the Split

My responsibilities were fairly easy to separate on paper. I could sort them under the headings of teacher and administrator. I could not make the distinction, as easily, in my lived reality. I consciously brought both teaching and administrative perspectives to bear as Robert and I attempted to solve problems in the operation of the school. I sought to see both sides of the problem, reflecting on the way in which the problem was affecting both teachers and administration, attempting to find a solution acceptable to both sides. When I shared my concerns, I found that my experience was not Robert's. He did not find himself torn in two different directions as did I. For Robert it appeared relatively straightforward, as he cautioned me,

> "You are walking with one foot in administration and another in teaching. You can't be in administration and teaching, too!" He says that this will prove dangerous, and that I will eventually have to make a choice as to my loyalties. (Journal entry, spring 1993)

> I was shocked by Robert's remark.

> I wonder if he feels this way, because he is a full-time administrator? Has he been away from the classroom too long? Does he really think of administration and teaching as separate functions? Are we not all teachers? Does it have to be as Robert says? (Journal entry, spring 1993)

Robert was not telling me that as an administrator I could not teach, but recognizing that there are inherent tensions in the split role of teacher/administrator. Ultimately I would have to choose which I wanted to be. Robert's experience of administration had taught him this.

As vice-principal, I live my teaching story on the in-classroom space on the landscape. On the out-of-classroom space, I want to live both my teaching story and my administration story. Can I live my stories of teaching and administration in harmony, without discord? Can I find a way to have them complement each other—blur the lines between my visions of teaching and administration? Or will I find, as Robert warned, that I must eventually make a choice—administrator or teacher?

CHAPTER 13

Learning to Dance
in Administration: A Two-Step
in Professional Development

Sheila Dermer Applebaum and Jinjiang Du

The following story takes place in the Adult English as a Second Language (ESL) Center, located inside Chapel Secondary School. This school is in an older area of Toronto, fairly close to major intersections but still in a quiet neighborhood. It is built of cement slabs and is a functional efficient-looking building—not one you would immediately associate with a board of education school. On the outside, it has an institutional look; on the inside, it is bright and airy. The front of it has a two-story window, displaying a greenhouse. Plants growing above the door create a friendly-looking entrance. The doors are big and heavy—seemingly made for adults rather than children. Outside, the students in their midteens are milling about, shy one moment and fooling around the next. They all come from new immigrant families of various ethnocultural backgrounds, a constant reminder of the community that our adult ESL educators serve. Often, these students come into the school about the same time as our own ESL staff, competing for space as they run up the stairs to avoid being late.

The Adult ESL Administration Center is on the second floor. Although housed in the school building, the center is, in fact, very different in function and feels separate from the rest of the secondary school. At one end of the center, the small library, well stocked with multiple copies of adult-ESL and management texts, accommodates a couple of tables, chairs and a couch. It is easily accessible for instructors and lead instructors when they drop in at their leisure. At the other end, the support staff welcomes new immigrants and refers them to appropriate programs throughout the city. As administrator, I always leave my door open for easier communication with the staff.

141

I am in the midst of preparing for a meeting with lead instructors who are supervisors of numerous ESL instructors in adult and continuing education. Morale has been rather low all year because of the recent government legislation forcing restructuring and reduction of our programs. Aware of the recognized marginality of adult education, everyone keeps wondering if we are simply going to be the next target on the chopping block. Would ESL and continuing education become the rejected players of a school system following its own rules of a children's game: "Last one in; first one out!"? Today, the lead instructors are looking for direction from me as their administrator, about the established practice of performing everyday organizational tasks such as visiting instructors and writing instructor reports. As part of their role as lead instructors, they seem to want reassurance that their voices and those of their instructors are being heard beyond the classroom. I could see such an assurance in this disheartening environment would be especially significant to them. It was these regular monthly visits to their instructors' classes and subsequent reports that provided the contextual backdrop for our meeting's agenda.

Under its administration, the Adult ESL Center delivers various types and levels of ESL curriculum, offered on different schedules to suit the needs of the diverse ethnocultural communities. The operation of the ESL classes is monitored and supervised by lead instructors, both in schools and in community agencies. They have office space at the center, but usually work according to their own schedules, traveling from one place to the next in the city, visiting approximately 300 classes. There is a weekly group meeting intended to provide support and to maintain uniformity in program and administration. Some of the recent meetings had turned out to be an arena for shadow boxing. On one side was the administration, who wanted the curriculum guidelines implemented by the lead instructors through workshops and paired conversations with their instructors. On the other side was some instructional staff, who resisted these activities as outside their job description and demanded remuneration for in-service. The tension between those who created the curriculum implementation procedure and those who had to enact it was increasing. Both lead instructors and instructors were flexing their muscles in staying their ground. Consequently, I was looking for an opportunity through staff development to ease this onerous situation.

The ESL lead instructors had been following the procedure of visiting instructors and writing reports for several years as directed by administration and the instructors' collective agreement. When a special topic such as staff development about instructor reports is added to a regular lead instructors' meeting like this, notes are sometimes written that help us reflect on what went right or wrong and what was unexpected. This time I asked a lead instructor, Jinjiang Du, whom I had been dialogue-journaling with for several months, if he would also be interested in writing his impressions about this meeting. He seemed to welcome the challenge and opportunity to be heard by management. I looked forward to counterpointing our voices in terms of the same activity. It was obvious that decision making by authority without discussion was not working; it was important to find a better method.

Jinjiang begins his story:

> It was Tuesday morning at Chapel Adult ESL Center. As usual, when there was a lead instructors' meeting scheduled, all lead instructors gathered in their room across from the main office, well before 10:30 a.m. Nobody seemed to care about the seating arrangement. Most of us were already seated along the two long tables that were stretched out from end to end in the middle of the room between the leads' desks, leaving the two ends of the tables visibly unoccupied. Everyone was just waiting for Sheila, who we knew was still at a meeting with the clerical staff. As she was working greatly reduced hours because of a study leave, she was supposed to tackle whatever came into her hands as efficiently as possible. It became so important for us at such a meeting to make a selective and condensed report of the individual matters each of us had for solution or confirmation.
>
> But we all knew there was going to be something more today before the routine give- and -take took place. High on the agenda today was Sheila's feedback on our monthly class visit reports. (Journal entry, J. D., November 1995)

In a similar way, my own journal entry concerning the start of this meeting reflected Jinjiang's. However, I was more consciously aware of the meaning of our space and my desire to create a kind of symmetry—a certain receptive yet productive mood.

> It was 10:30 in the morning when I entered the lead instructors' room. Two lengthy tables were standing in the middle of the room between the rows of leads' desks on each side. Usually, the leads ate their lunches or snacks there. The tables were stretched out end to end as I tried to find a side position. Only the seat at the head of the tables was available—supposedly the administrator's spot for giving out information. Trying to avoid this organizational deference, I asked for help in putting the tables side by side to form a small square. Immediately one lead casually said to another: "That's much better for our discussion—we can all see each other when we talk." A modest respectful acknowledgment of each person's voice. (Journal entry, S. D. A., November 1995)

In a later journal entry, Jinjiang assesses this procedure of completing instructor reports. He thinks there are "very few guidelines as to how to make [their] reports satisfactorily serve the purpose" (journal entry, December 1995). For several years apparently, the lead instructors have felt that although this procedure during class visits had emanated from the instructors' collective agreement, it has been distanced from its previous historical, narrative context. They viewed this procedure as a ritualized event and a "rhetoric of conclusions" (Clandinin & Connelly, 1995, p. 11). That is to say, genuine collaboration concerning the rationale and way for carrying out supervision was initially not an expressed consideration by management. The lead instructors were never included in a discussion about class visits or writing monthly reports.

The moral dilemma that presents itself is that lead instructors are caught between carrying out policy regarding the monitoring of instructors through monthly class visits and confronting their administrator about the value of such a prescriptive task. One afternoon I overheard the following remark: "Sometimes the routine visits are so dull that the writing of reports seems to lead nowhere at all." As a partial solution to this ennui, the leads submitted their monthly instructor reports to me for an "informal" evaluation. Meanwhile, I was trying to create an opportunity for "teacher talk" outside the classrooms where they act as supervisors and write reports about their instructors.

Jinjiang writes:

> I was a little anxious. Like the rest of them, I had my notebook and planner ready in front of me, prepared to take down whatever instruction or comment Sheila would issue in a moment. Although it was not sheer admonishment that I was anticipating, somehow I sensed that I would hear more negative criticism than positive from our boss this time.
>
> Then, much to my surprise, Sheila didn't mention her checklist of criteria for effective visits that enumerated her expectations of us. Neither did she seem to even want to make a direct comment on our monthly reports as such. Apparently she had changed her strategy. In a manner of negotiation, Sheila tactfully suggested that maybe each of us should think of a best visit experience and share this story with the rest of the group.

In terms of the professional knowledge landscape, the lead instructors' desire to create their own opportunity for professional development brought them together with their administrator for this evaluation meeting. But without a rigid plan in hand, this meeting developed into a different type of professional development which did not come via the conduit.

Jinjiang continues his story:

> It took a few minutes for us to reorganize our thoughts—we were asked to be productive now rather than to be passively receptive! I

surely had a lot to tell, but I hadn't come to this meeting to tell everyone what great work I had done, had I?

I began to trust my intuition. I was trying to make sense of my work in assessing the lead instructors in the same way that they were evaluating their own instructors. What was the genuine educative purpose of their monthly visits? They were trying to understand the parallels between learning to participate in this staff development meeting and sharing an instructor's teaching experience and milieu during a monthly visit. Any suggestions about visiting their instructors and writing meaningful reports would initially be modeled by how I evaluated their reports at this meeting and how I treated them as professionals—not only by words but by intention. Although it had sometimes been distressing to face the paradox between my intentions and how they were perceived by my staff, I fully recognized the ways that hierarchical structures in a large organization foster this distrust. It appeared that future implementation of their responsibilities would be influenced by the blend of their past experiences and the kind of messages communicated from this meeting.

I then questioned who these visits were really for. We needed to identify the stakeholders for these reports. How could we ensure who would derive benefit from them? The lead instructors and their instructors were a team whose primary interests seemed to be unfocused until now. Sometimes, writing the report was taking precedence over the importance of the shared experience between them. As a group, the lead instructors needed to understand their experiences in the context of their role as service providers of effective adult-ESL programs. They needed to know how they were constructing their knowledge and how it was being shared in practice with their instructors. Just like teachers having to learn from their own experiences, I also had to start from the leads' expertise; they seemed to feel it was not sufficiently acknowledged by the board as an organization. My orderly checklist of criteria for "how to make a successful class visit and instructor report" would become a secondary consideration. During this transitional period of uncertainty, we all wondered whether the evolving sense of transformation from routine to renewed commitment to teacher development would ever be experienced outside the doors of our meeting.

In the beginning it was difficult to sit back and just listen to them without comment. I had been a lead instructor for several years and could empathize directly with their professional concerns. In addition, the lead instructors were pushing to copy my now popular list of "how-to's" for writing visit reports. However, I wanted them to acknowledge the validity of their visits experientially, by reflecting on their own teaching and supervisory background. Just like asking an instructor, "How do you think the lesson went?" "What were you trying to accomplish?" I now wanted to hear the stories retold from their classroom visits.

Jinjiang continues his observation of the meeting:

> Paula was the first one to tell her story. What she tried to share with us was her experience with an ESL class when her assumption about a certain teaching method turned out to be incorrect.
>
> The class was doing WH-question practice (What? Where? When?) through a game play. At first I thought that the way they did it wouldn't work with such a mixed group. The instructor was definitely not following the traditional way of dealing with grammar when learners were of such mixed proficiency levels. (Lead instructors' meeting, November 21, 1995)

Her first reaction as lead instructor was to point out the gap in this instructor's pedagogy. But she held back and listened carefully to the interaction around her.

> Obviously I was in the wrong frame of mind! Later I saw lots of WH-questions coming back again naturally from the learners. I realized it was good methodology. I had been wrong in my assumption that only one way brought recognizable results. My double take on what happened in class helped me see things differently in the future. How instructors were coming to know what worked for their learners in spite of the textbook examples was an avenue for us as lead instructors to share with them.

Exploring alternative methods of teaching and listening to the teachers' voice were clearly ways of providing supervision through demonstrated collaboration.

> Paula was so absorbed in her thoughts while recounting her story that she began going into unnecessary details. Sheila had to cut it short due to the time limit. But the starting of this storytelling process immediately turned into a warm and relaxing interaction in the group. I could see Sheila beaming with excitement as she listened and later made comment on Paula's openness to surprise during her visit.
>
> "Sheila may not have expected such a positive turn with this meeting," I thought to myself.
>
> Cathy then told of her rewarding experience of caring for her instructors.
>
> When we do classroom visits, what we encounter is not always with curriculum and teaching. Our instructors may have other problems.

Gilligan (1982) describes a morality of care and responsibility that fits this professional knowledge landscape. Although this voice is not limited by gender, but rather by theme, it predominates in women. It values attachment, care, and engagement as primary bases for moral decisions. Cathy was expressing the responsibility for her instructor within this framework of caring.

Cathy continues:

> On a recent visit, the instructor I saw had just experienced the sudden death of a student in her other class. She appeared so distraught and wanted desperately to talk to somebody. I realized she was having emotional problems besides this. So I listened to her. My interest in what she had to tell me seemed to make her feel better. In a practical way, I also directed her to seek counseling and gave her the telephone number.

Like Jinjiang and his female colleagues, Cathy was capable of using both a caring and an objective voice to solve a moral issue.

Jinjiang tells his own story:

> When my turn came, I chose to tell about my joy in seeing an instructor's improvement following a serious and sincere exchange of ideas. An instructor had complained more than once that much to her despair, her students wouldn't stop using their bilingual dictionary in class. I listened to her and expressed appreciation of her attempt to wean the students from relying almost totally on their first language. We both accepted the conceptual notion that ESL learners should be encouraged to use their first language to facilitate their understanding of difficult English concepts. Meanwhile, I pointed out that there was nothing wrong with using a dictionary. What was important was to offer them a good alternative and to guide them to the right track to promote growth and independence. So I recommended a couple of good English dictionaries suitable for ESL learners.
>
> On a later visit, I saw some students already using dictionaries suggested by the instructor. She was also busily taking pains to encourage them to make the best of the dictionary. "They use their little (bilingual) dictionary much less often now," she said with a proud smile. Of course, her openness to change made me feel good too!
>
> By the time all the stories were told, about half the items on Sheila's checklist had been mentioned naturally through our dialogue. In her summation, Sheila said she was thrilled by what happened at this meeting. I believe she really was. In fact, I was thrilled too. And probably so were most of my colleagues. Although none of us obtained the actual checklist until later, I felt pretty good about my work. I am pretty sure how I can do my work better.

The opportunity to share these professional stories with others helped to enhance the possibilities for planning teacher development through collaborative supervision. It reinforced their confidence in dealing with the same instructors from another perspective. They had a chance to recognize that the mutuality of purpose in their relationship with their instructors would determine the meaningfulness of what was discussed and shared through their visits.

In the end, this mode of sharing confronted the sacred theory-practice story as it normally discloses itself in professional development. Instead of only relying on their administrator or on experts in the field, they began to rely on themselves—their own experience and knowledge. Would this shift in approach and competing story to the sacred story of professional development be valued by instructors and superintendents within the system? Would it be acceptable to promote lead instructor "teacher-talk" as a way of knowing, without calling the staff development trainers? Lead instructors sometimes are made to feel that their knowledge is not complete—as if they will always be learners who need to be taught by experts both in ESL and management areas; as if only one more university course or training session might help. On this particular day, they began to feel that their group meeting and interaction were "more than just another way of doing professional development but were, instead, representative of a new sense of what it means to be professional" (Clandinin & Connelly, 1995, p. 126). This was an opportunity for the lead instructors to talk about their actual experiences and feelings in the classrooms where they visited each month to observe, participate, or demonstrate a lesson. This was a chance to discuss what really mattered on a daily basis with their instructors on the professional knowledge landscape.

Through their storytelling and collaboration, visiting classes and writing reports were becoming less prescriptive and more meaningful activities. Discussing the rationale and relevant policies removed some of the previous abstraction. It led instead to a critical reflection on their behavior as supervisors and to a retelling of their own stories. It disclosed how much their personal desire for professional recognition was similar to their instructors' need to be valued as professionals. It also revealed to me that part of a leader's effectiveness is influenced by the language that she shares with her colleagues and by the extent to which she can explain and thereby give order to their collective experiences (Van Maanen, 1988). Using popular organizational terms such as *collaboration* only has meaning when they are constructed together as part of a relationship. The tension of lead instructors struggling for this sense of voice was partly dissipated by the increasing awareness of what their role embodied and what they wanted it to be—both with their administrator and their instructors.

As in other large educational institutions, sacred theory-practice stories persist—lead instructors are obliged to follow board policy and procedures as they are funneled through the organization. But now, through their class visits and discussion, there seemed to be an opportunity for a truly educative experience with their instructors—a sense of personal growth and caring relationships from our unplanned professional development.

Jinjiang concludes his observation of the meeting:

> When the meeting was over, one of the leads suggested that we keep the tables in a square as they now stood, and leave the other half of the room empty. "So we can dance over there!" I said. Everybody laughed.

CHAPTER 14

Life on the Professional Knowledge Landscape: Living the "Principal as Rebel" Image

Cheryl Craig

Recently, I worked at Meadowlark School, where I came to know Allan, the principal. During my time at the school, I could see that Allan influenced school practices and people through expressing a particular image of the principalship in his administrative practices. I begin this chapter with a discussion of how I first experienced Allan enacting his rebel image at Meadowlark. Next, I introduce his biography and hone in on particular incidents that contributed to the development of his "principal as rebel" image. I then feature the knowledge communities that have sustained Allan over time and finish with a reflective turn on the professional knowledge landscape and its hope for the future.

Allan: "Principal as Rebel"

In staff meetings, professional development days, interviews, and private conversations, I came to see that Allan held the image of principal as rebel and enacted it in his leadership practices. I also came to understand that Allan felt "lonely" as a principal and needed someone with whom to discuss his work.

I began my participant observation sessions at Meadowlark Elementary School in January 1991 but I was not highly visible in the school until mid-May. I had preliminary conversations with Allan in January, but our relationship did not develop until I was consistently in the school and visibly in relationship with some of the 28 staff members. Allan often initiated conversations with me, as I did with him. I believe that we communicated mutually in ways that probed the deeper meanings we held for our practices.

In June, Allan described his image of principal as rebel to me, an image that continued to punctuate our conversations and Allan's leadership practices. Allan described rebels as "people who think a little differently than mainstream people," people who "do not swallow hook, line, and sinker everything they are told in the school system." He considers the rebel as something that "lives inside of him" and believes it lives to varying degrees inside the principals with whom he associates. As a rebel, Allan believes that "people should have freedom to think and freedom to make changes . . . freedom to do what *people* think is right." When Allan shared his knowledge with me, I became curious about the sense he was making of his administrative experiences in different places on the professional knowledge landscape.

At first, it seemed to me that Allan was checking me out to see if his views were safe with me:

> He questioned me about what was important [in the practice of education]. I said I wanted to do things with which I morally agreed. I wanted the things I do to be in the best interests of students and teachers. In the end, I said I needed to please myself because I had to live with the things I do in my career and their impact on others.

After my response, I had the feeling that Allan saw me as a person he could trust: "I could tell by his body language and his comments I was answering his questions in the way he would like."

In our interactions, I came to more fully understand Allan as a principal and how his enactments of his image impacted school practices and the knowledge constructions/reconstructions of the Meadowlark teachers. I came to see that Allan called forth his rebel image in response to something he was having difficulty naming in his experiences. At first glance, it seemed to me that he was rebelling against the school system. A more careful reading of Allan's practices, however, showed that he was rebelling against something else—something that Clandinin and Connelly (1995) describe as a sacred theory-practice story whose theory-driven plot line shapes the landscape that educators come to know.

One way Allan lived his rebel image was in his hiring practices. Towards the end of my first year at Meadowlark, a resource teacher was needed to fill a vacancy and an experienced person was recommended by system officials. I noted:

> I can see [Allan] is open to having a newcomer fill the position. He talks of fresh ideas and fresh possibilities with much the same passion

as he talks about beginning teachers. Allan is not bound to entrenched beliefs about seniority and experience in the school system.

Allan did not choose the individual he was expected to hire, but hired a teacher within the school. His rebel image guided and drove his actions, spurring him to ignore a "should" outlined by those above him in the conduit.

Allan also expressed his rebel image when he protected a beginning teacher on temporary contract. If he had adhered to staffing guidelines, the beginning teacher would have been replaced by a tenured teacher. Allan, however, disagreed with beginning teachers being "bounced from school to school," a practice he felt was "not healthy for beginning teachers or the school system." Over the summer months, he penciled the beginning teacher into a position left open by a teacher who, on Allan's recommendation, had not yet declared her maternity leave. As a result, the beginning teacher was not declared surplus until the fall. Then, before the move was to take place, Allan found a staff member who was required to have high-needs school experience to become an administrator. That teacher took the transfer and the beginning teacher retained his position at Meadowlark School. In this situation, Allan worked outside staffing regulations, finding an alternate way to solve a twisty situation. Again, he relied on personal knowledge rather than on conduit-sanctioned procedures.

Because Allan viewed situations differently from school system officials, he understood why he was never selected to sit on high-profile committees dealing with policy formation or administrative appointments. Although Allan had seniority, he was excluded from committees because "[he] did not espouse the prevailing ideology." If Allan were placed on committees, he would choose people who would do jobs well, "not because they know how to play the game." He pointed to the example of a former staff member who applied for a leadership position. Because he knew her qualifications and experience, he inquired into why she was not appointed. "She knows too much" was the response he received. Allan came to the disturbing realization that the individual was being denied a position because she voiced new ways in which to live on the landscape. He found it difficult to excuse this practice.

Another situation that perturbed Allan was when his staff members were short-listed for administrative appointments at the beginning of the school year. Certain teachers and administrators were scheduled for interviews with no respect for the "community-building" sessions planned at the school level. Despite the interruptions, Allan did not blame the short-listed individuals:

> For all we talk about cooperation and collaboration, it [the school system] is in fact a competition. . . . It is each person for themselves.

When the individuals came to talk about their [interviews], I said: "You do what is best for you."

In rebel fashion, Allan openly voiced his concerns about school system procedures with staff members.

He particularly pointed to the career ladder, a business notion transplanted into the field of education. The career ladder, in Allan's view, was a prime example of an individual, as opposed to a community, pursuit.

At the same time as the school system excluded Allan from key decision-making committees, he limited the school system's impact on his school and his staff. Allan's rebel image particularly came to the fore one professional development day as he worked with teachers:

> I noticed how Allan . . . let the staff carry the discussion . . . The times he said anything that revealed himself were in resisting mandates: the number of minutes of instruction for Grade 1 students . . . and the decree that every school have a sign-in book.

The mandate that schools have teacher attendance books particularly upset a teacher who felt the move detracted from teachers' professionalism. Allan responded: "We have got by without using it . . . and I think we can continue the old way." At the same time as Allan protected certain practices, he held others open for scrutiny. Of the teachers' handbooks that every teacher kept updated with policies, he said, "It's just a myriad of material; my question is, how useful is it?" As for a mandated "school improvement plan," Allan vetoed it in my first year at Meadowlark and verbally submitted what was to be a written plan in my 2nd year.

Allan also enacted his rebel image by intentionally filtering information being funneled into the school by the school system. One particular instance stands out. At the beginning of the school year, Allan, like all other administrators, attended a system speech and was expected to share the address with teachers. He said he would pass along information if it had to do with stress, because "stress is a real problem . . . teachers have a tendency to overwork. . . . There is a fair amount of absenteeism at peak stress periods." On the other hand, if the speech contained moral admonitions about what teachers should be doing or "big words" imported from places such as California or Oregon, he would ignore it because it added to teachers' stress levels. In the end, he shielded the Meadowlark teachers from the speech because he considered it a "stressor." Allan would not be drawn into transmitting messages and language he could not support.

I turn now to my most recent work with Allan and highlight his biography. I show how particular incidents contributed to the development of his rebel image and illustrate their connections to the sacred theory-practice story.

Allan's Biography

Allan grew up in a small town on the outskirts of a major Canadian city. He entered the teaching profession, not because he felt compelled to be an educator, but because he was counseled into the profession. He attended university in a nearby city and became a physical education teacher. When he entered the teaching profession in the 1960s, there was lots of "societal turmoil and change" and "lots of questioning." Allan was cultivated at a time when innovations flourished and in a context where it was "OK to question" conventional educational practices. The conduit was much less sophisticated in his early years and the principal position was more turned toward service. During the span of Allan's career, however, the numbers of administrators in the school system has dramatically increased, as have the number of people consulting to schools. Furthermore, Allan has witnessed kindergarten being formally integrated into the school system, special education becoming increasingly specialized, a rampant increase in individuals conducting psychological tests and assessments, and an increase in technical support specialists to schools. These significant increases in positions reflect the growth of administration as a profession as well as a growth of specialization in fields such as curriculum, psychology, and technology. Taken together, they have added to the complexity of the career ladder and formed the backdrop to Allan's career on the landscape.

Allan first became acquainted with positions within the school system hierarchy in his first year of teaching. At that time, male and female teachers ate in separate lunchrooms. He entered the men's lunchroom and saw two leather chairs and several wooden chairs. Allan decided to sit on a leather chair. I turn to his telling:

> The principal came in and said: "Allan, that chair is reserved for the principal." [Allan] then walked around to sit on the other leather chair and the principal said, "Well, Allan, that one is reserved for the assistant principal." [Allan] then asked: "Which chair may I sit in?" The principal said: "Any of the other chairs would be fine."

Relegated to a wooden chair, Allan figured out the position of beginning teachers and teachers in general, a place that "never varied" in the years he was in the school. He also came in contact with the leather chairs, symbols of position in the conduit. While Allan admired the principal for his efficient way of managing the school, he questioned his way of working with people. He and the assistant principal often discussed their feeling of being "functionaries," technically fulfilling duties outlined by the conduit; not professional educators, people with knowledge who were capable of shaping their own futures. Memories of these initial experiences have remained with him and "niggled away" at him as his career has unfolded.

Allan ran into difficulty with the same principal on another occasion. The principal believed that schools should provide teacher-supervised lunchrooms, an abstract notion parachuted in from Great Britain. Allan, on the other hand, believed that teachers were doing too much:

> I was already spending an hour and a half to 2 hours a day on extracurricular activities. . . . We [the principal and I] got into an exchange, probably 10 to 15 minutes of discussion. Finally, the principal got upset and walked out. . . . He . . . stomped down the hallway as hard as his Hush Puppies would allow him.

The principal's reaction shocked Allan and he turned to the assistant principal for a reading of the situation:

> The assistant principal . . . said: "Ah, Allan, now you have done it. You have made the old boy angry." [Allan] replied: "What for? I thought we were having a discussion. . . ." He said, "No, Allan, you were not having a discussion, you were having an argument. He viewed it that way and your viewpoint was not acceptable."

Allan became involved in this argument because he did not understand that it was inappropriate to debate the sacred story. Only later did he discover that people who posed questions were storied as difficult. He did not understand that he could not question the principal. In his estimation, it took him 10 years to figure out that to publicly question someone above him in the hierarchy was to question their authority. His slow learning "cost" him because he was seen as someone "who did not follow the dictates." To further complicate matters, the school system was considerably smaller (over 100 fewer schools than the present time) and people such as his first principal were "kingmakers":

> A kingmaker is a principal at a school where you work. If you wanted to get into administration, you could do it through the old boys' network and the physical education department. Every assistant principal that went through my first school with that principal became a principal in a couple of years. . . . The principal hobnobbed

with the superintendents and they got together socially and had their little groups.

Whereas people around him became administrators, Allan did not. He remained in a teaching position much longer than his male colleagues.

About the same time as Allan discovered there were kingmakers in the school system, he also realized that there were "grey ghosts." I turn to his explanation:

> There is an empire that has been built very carefully and it contains what I call the grey ghosts in our system. These people know extremely well how the system works. . . . Some are supervisors, others consultants, people who have been around for a number of years. These people know where to be and what to say and who to talk to in order to ensure they will never end up in schools. . . . Any time you have a bureaucracy set up, those grey ghosts know how it works and they survive. They do a good job of it.

The empire Allan mentions is a way of referring to the conduit; the grey ghosts, the people with specializations; and their knowledge, knowledge of how the sacred story works. He further explained what he came to know about the functions of grey ghosts on the landscape:

> These people are shock absorbers. They pass things on. . . . They filter. . . . The problem is these people get puffed up with their pseudo-importance. . . . It bothers me when they import a message from Oregon or California or somewhere else. We capture it, massage it a bit, then say we are on the leading edge.

Early in his career, Allan saw the grey ghosts acquiring theory-driven practice from elsewhere, transporting it back to the school system, repackaging it, and funneling it onto the landscape as practical prescriptions. It bothered him how the grey ghosts set themselves up as knowers and justified their positions by sifting through research and development activities that originated elsewhere.

In 1969–1970, Allan was involved in "an ideal school" committee, a group of teachers who met to imagine what an ideal school might be like. The committee approached a superintendent and requested that they be placed in a high needs, inner-city school where they could put their ideals into practice. Allan explained what happened:

> I went to the inner city school as an assistant principal. I was only able to get one of the other people in the group to come with me in

5 years. . . . Only one other male . . . and unfortunately he only lasted 6 months because the students were very difficult to work with. . . . He left teaching.

Allan became an administrator when there was a rapid growth in the city's population, a time when the school system, in his opinion, "scraped bottom" to find male educators to appoint to administrative and consulting positions. Our conversation shifted to what Allan learned from this early experience as an assistant principal:

C: So what did that tell you about the school system's support for visions of ideal schools?
A: There was not any support. . . . I mean you did not have a vision unless it was perceived to be something that fit in . . .
C: But if it came . . .
A: Well, if it came from the top . . . you went along with it.
C: So, you were coming in with a new idea but you were not in the right niche?
A: Well, I was not in the right ideology. To me, that was the key.

Our conversation continued:

C: So your ideology was more in the ideal, the possible. . . . What was the school system's ideology?
A: Well, I think that ideology was to maintain the status quo . . . keep doing things we have always done and carry on.

This experience taught Allan that he and the people with whom he planned could not plug ideas into the conduit; only grey ghosts sanctioned by the conduit could do that. Beneath the guise of progress, however, he tacitly knew that nothing had changed in the plotline of the sacred story.

Allan believed the school system left him in an inner-city school for 5 years to teach him the following lesson:

A: If we put him in an inner-city school, fooling around with kids who are not really important, we will show him how the world really works and what real life is like. . . .
C: And he will fall back on track?
A: Right . . . but I didn't. . . . Everything I learned in that school . . . from those children and from their parents has served me well in the future.

Allan was placed in the inner-city school to reflect on how to think and act in ways deemed appropriate by those in the conduit. But Allan created his own knowledge from the experience and learned how to survive as an individual in an institution demanding conformity.

> I learned how . . . the inner-city people survive extremely well. They don't fit in with the norm but they have their own support group. . . . The interesting thing was they were expected to live that way. But not me . . . no, no, no. . . . Not as an administrator. I was an assistant principal. . . . I had done all the things you are supposed to do in addition to this learning process in an inner city community.

Allan realized that he could protect his individuality by appearing to be a conformist. He could live a cover story because he, for the most part, behaved appropriately as an administrator. Our conversation continued:

C: So you kind of learned a guise, a cover. . . .
A: That's right. . . .
C: . . . the cover or the guise was what the school system hierarchy needed to see to advance you?
A: Oh, yes, that's right. They needed to feel comfortable. . . . They needed to know I could project the expectations. They needed to feel I could do it.

After working for 3 years in the inner-city school, Allan requested a transfer but was told: "No, we like you where you are." This comment has echoed back at Allan over the years and we discussed its meaning:

C: So what did that comment mean to you?
A: Well, to me, it meant: "Allan, don't make waves. Stay where you are. We will let you know when we think you are ready for a move."

Allan was again reminded that people above him decide his future, not he. He also came to know that his feelings and perceptions, part and parcel of his personal practical knowledge, were not valued.

In his 4th year in the inner-city school, Allan repeated his transfer request and received the same negative reply. By this time, he had come to know how that punishment can drive personnel practices in the conduit. In Allan's 5th year, a new superintendent offered him a choice between two different high needs schools. But the rebel in Allan replied: "No, this is not going to work. I need a change from high-needs schools."

After challenging the superintendent, Allan was offered an administrative position in a new school, a placement that brought with it a new dilemma. He had been placed with a principal who was a protégé of his first principal.

Furthermore, he and the new principal were both active in the Teachers' Association and had publicly expressed opposing viewpoints. Allan tells the story this way:

> Bob Williams [the principal with whom Allan had publicly disagreed] telephoned and said: "Allan, I would like to talk to you. . . . Have you talked to the superintendent yet?" [Allan] said, "Yes." He said: "I will come over to see you."

The principal came to Allan's school to share his interpretation of the situation: "Allan, central administration is laughing at us because we have not got along in the past [in the Teachers' Association]." Allan and Bob realized that they had been set up. Laying aside their hierarchical positions and their adversarial stances, Allan and Bob discovered common ground: deeply rooted beliefs in democratic process and staff participation.

While working with Bob, the superintendent who blocked Allan's transfer requests offered him a principalship. Allan was reluctant to accept it because he was learning so much from Bob. Furthermore, the new job would involve a lengthy commute. Allan's pause displeased the superintendent, who said: "You know, Allan, you have a reputation of being a bit difficult. If you want a principalship, this *one* is the *one* being offered." Out of the corner of his eye, Allan saw Bob prompting him to respond in the affirmative. It finally occurred to Allan that the conduit, which both gives and takes away positions, was offering him a job. He swallowed his protests and replied: "Oh, that's great, that's great, Mr. Crandall. Thank you so much. I will take it!"

The conversation surrounding Allan's first principalship, however, has remained etched in his memory. He explains:

> So that is how I got moved [into a principalship]. But again, you see, it [the notion of me being considered difficult] came back and I never forgot that: "Allan, you have a reputation of being difficult." But Bob never saw it that way.

While Bob enabled Allan to compose a competing story, the superintendent did not. The superintendent wanted Allan's enactments of his rebel image shut down. In the situation, Allan understood the risks to advancement associated with expressing his personal knowledge.

On becoming an administrator, Allan went to a workshop, part of "the indoctrination process," to become familiar with the policies and procedures of the school system. There, he found himself being filled up with knowledge of his place in the conduit and with correct responses to situations. One particular point proved memorable for Allan: "Planning leads to anti-planning." Allan formed his own interpretation of antiplanning and took it to mean "an alternate way of thinking . . . a better way of thinking." The notion fit with his developing image of principal as rebel:

> That [notion] stuck with me. . . . Once I know who is doing the planning, then I can antiplan. I can do what I need to do. . . . That became a dictum which has shaped my administrative practice.

Antiplanning has helped Allan figure out how the conduit works and ways to circumvent it. But, in spite of his tacit attempts to dislodge it, the sacred story underpinning the conduit has continued to flourish.

Midcareer, Allan again ran into trouble with a superintendent, one who had given a speech and asked for questions. Allan took the invitation seriously. This is his story of what happened:

> We were allowed to ask a few questions so I asked a couple of questions. I guess he [the superintendent] interpreted them as outstepping the bounds . . . the questions made him uncomfortable. He said: "If you can't stand the heat, get out of the kitchen." That was very meaningful to me. You see, I could stand the heat but he did not like me being in his kitchen. The remark, you know, was not only directed at me, it was meant for the over 100 people gathered there.

In this public forum, Allan and the other principals in the audience came to know what happens to middle-management administrators who are seen as overstepping their positions.

But Allan overstepped his position once more in his career, this time on a more recent occasion. He presented an alternate viewpoint when he had the rare opportunity to be a member of a committee examining administrative appointments. He was invited to be part of the committee, not because of his work in the system, but because of his leadership of an administrative group outside it. The committee was composed of high-ranking officials, three principals, and a female representative. I turn to Allan's description of the proceedings:

> A superintendent asked me about my perception and the perception of those with whom I work [about how promotions are made in the school system]. I said: "Well, our perceptions happen to be that if you don't follow the current ideology of the school system, you are not going to get promoted." You could have heard a pin drop . . . on the carpet.

Allan then took a reading of the other committee members' reactions:

I said it and the female representative looked at me with this amused smile on her face. Another principal sitting beside me nudged my chair because he knew exactly what I meant.

A further principal told him: "Al, they did not hear you," and I replied: "I do not care. It is there and I am going to articulate it." In rebel fashion, Allan voiced opinions concerning the career ladder that others dared not mention. The sanctity of the sacred story remained intact, however, because his remarks were met with silence.

Allan has repeatedly reflected on incidents such as this one and tried to make sense of them from the perspective of those in the conduit:

A: See when you put somebody in a position of authority, you have to trust them . . . that they are going to support you.
C: But that has been a bit of a challenge for you, though. . . .
A: That's right.
C: Because you voice your personal opinions, sometimes?
A: That's right. On an issue, that is right.

Allan tacitly knows that life in the conduit demands that he follow the "party line." He also understands that the authority of position prevails. Although he has figured these things out, he occasionally blows his cover by sharing personal responses instead of conduit-driven views. Our conversation continued:

C: But you would never pit yourself against administration. It was only when you felt strongly about something. . . .
A: That's right. I do not see myself as being anti-administration per se. . . . I was just expressing my point of view. . . .
C: On certain things . . . and occasionally it would run you counter to other people?
A: Exactly. I feel very strongly even today that it is important to question and present alternate viewpoints.

Allan's desire to present alternate views is grounded in his beliefs in participatory democracy. In attempting to live a democratic life, though, Allan has, on occasion, found himself at loggerheads with people in central administration. His intentions were never to be against system leadership per se. Yet, it has been convenient for some to story his actions that way.

Having portrayed Allan's interactions over time in out-of-school places on the landscape, I now turn to his interactions in in-school places and focus on his relationships with the staff at Meadowlark.

In direct opposition to people above them in the conduit, Meadowlark teachers embrace Allan's way of being. They find him open to teachers and students who view things differently. Rather than silencing people who question school practices, Allan encourages, even invites, questions. He describes his typical response to a person challenging his thinking:

> When someone asks questions of me, I listen, I reflect, I clarify . . . I say, "Tell me more." I consider what the person is telling me and check back to see if I have got their message. I also check to see if I have made my meaning clear. I consider whether I need to refine my thinking.

Allan uses alternate thinking to refine his thoughts and his practices and when dictates do wind their way through the conduit, he takes the stance that

> it behooves me to say, "Look, is there another way? Are there other ways of thinking? Are there better ways to do this or perhaps there is not, who knows?"

Allan attempts to co-construct a context at Meadowlark School where different perspectives can be shared:

> So when I work with the staff and they come in and say: "Allan, we think this, we think that," I always keep alternate thinking, anti-planning in mind and say: "Yes, why not? Your ideas are just as good as mine. . . ." In many cases, teachers' ideas are better because they are dealing directly with the children and they know curriculum and stuff like that.

Allan's deep respect for teachers and their knowledge has earned him the reputation of being considered an "amazingly collaborative" principal:

A: I may be viewed as being collaborative because I hold the view that if someone else has an idea, they should be able to bring it forward. . . .
C: You give teachers a space to share their ideas?
A: Oh, of course. My job is to be a facilitator, to help them do the things they believe to be best. . . .

C: Not the person bringing back ideas from the school system?
A: . . . Oh, no.

Allan's desire to help people do what they believe to be best as opposed to following the plotline of the sacred story has been both a source of pleasure and pain for him. In a conversation concerning what "being difficult" means, Allan explains how he has come to terms with this double-edged sword:

A: You asked me to explain "difficult" to those above me. . . . It was very simple. You ask too many questions.
C: People who question are difficult?
A: Yes, that is right. . . . But it has been very positive for me in the end. . . . I can say, "Allan, you have never really played the game of ingratiating yourself to someone for personal gain."
C: So whatever came your way came through you?
A: That's correct. Absolutely . . . "To Thine Own Self Be True." . . . That almost sounds trite but it is deeply important to me to be able to reflect on my career and consider what I've done as an accomplishment . . . because I have done things *with* and *for* people . . . not *to* people or asked things *of* people.
C: And you derive a great sense of personal integrity from this?
A: That's correct, exactly. . . . That is how I have made peace with my career.

Reflecting on his career from beginning to present, Allan relates his questioning to his job satisfaction and his ability to maintain personal integrity. From these qualities, he derives a sense of peace.

Having shared my work with Allan over a 4-year period, I turn now to examining how he has sustained himself on a landscape that he has found inhospitable at times. I address this query in the next section, where I present Allan's communities of sustenance, his knowledge communities.

Communities of Sustenance

In previous work, I have described knowledge communities as the individuals and groups of people with whom educators make sense of their practices. Whereas relationships in the conduit are imposed by the hierarchy of position and the hierarchy of knowledge, relationships in knowledge communities are naturally formed around "commonplaces of human experience"

(Lane, 1988). Outside the influence of the conduit, knowledge communities are secure places where educators share their knowledge. I now introduce Allan's multiple knowledge communities. An examination of these communities offers insights into how he has continued his expressions of his rebel image on the conduit-driven landscape.

"All along," explains Allan, "I have had colleagues [who have] offer[ed] me alternatives from their practical experiences. It has always been important to me to access the thinking of my colleagues." As he made references to people in his knowledge communities in our conversations, I realized that one knowledge community included an individual who has been with him since his university days. Employed by the same school board and both administrators, they have continued to log in with one another over the decades. Some of the members of the "ideal school" committee in the 1970s also form part of the knowledge community groups to which he belongs. They also have sustained him over a lengthy period of time. I now focus on Allan's present communities of knowing.

Allan currently has six individuals and three informally organized groups outside the conduit with whom he shares his knowledge. Four of the individuals are also part of one of the groups to which he belongs but since Allan and they have a common life outside the groups, they constitute knowledge communities in their own right.

One of the groups with whom Allan associates is a group whom the individuals call the Renaissance Resisters. Allan meets these people every 6–8 weeks to talk about the "ills of the system, how things could change, be changed. . . . We flatter ourselves but we do it with our colleagues, people who are in our shoes." He goes on to explain: "We are a renaissance people who talk about philosophical things. It is an opportunity to have a good time, to talk, and support each other." Allan has met with these individuals in an organized fashion over the past 5 years and they have recently made their association public. The informal name the group has chosen for itself is very telling. First, it resonates with Allan's "rebel image." Second, the word *renaissance* suggests a cultural rebirth, a return to a time when people and their aesthetic, moral, artistic, spiritual, and personal selves flourished. This also makes sense because Allan and his colleagues would feel more comfortable on a landscape similar to the one where Allan and many of his colleagues were cultivated in the 1960s, a landscape where inquiry was supported as a part of democratic life. The name, "Renaissance Resisters," with its reference to philosophical discussions, takes us back to the Greeks and Plato (and incidentally explains a common T-shirt that they wear), but it suggests something else as well. Historically, the Renaissance is also known as a time of enlightenment. One of the legacies of this particular historical time is the belief that human beings could contribute to the shaping of their lives, that they were not only shaped by external forces. Along with this legacy came a belief in the centrality of human reason and an introduction to the view of knowledge as humanly constructed and contextualized. This description is also apt because Allan and his colleagues enact their personal knowledge which they have constructed and reconstructed in context and circumvent knowledge delivered to them by the conduit. I return now to Allan's description of the individuals with whom he exchanges stories:

> Each of us have had ripples. . . . The common thing is that each of us has bucked the system . . . several times. David has gone up against violence, school program, busing, wellness. He is knowledgable in all those areas, but his talk has not been accepted. Martin always questions. Meetings become quiet when he makes his viewpoint known. People nod, even those who normally do not agree with him. George has questioned excessive fire regulations that severely limit the display of student work in schools. He finds little ways to go against the grain. Brian has an amazing ability to move through many groups, planting alternate ideas. Roger is a good thinker. He has a remarkable ability to say something and people agree with it. When they stop to think, they realize he has told them their ideas are a pile of malarkey. We provide alternatives. We are not against everything.

Although Allan does not describe the full membership of this particular knowledge community, he gives us a flavor for their commonalties and the texts that they share. It is apparent that each individual has had ripples because they have asked questions, provided alternate viewpoints, planted competing ideas, challenged people in the conduit and the sacred story itself. Like Allan, the people in this knowledge community maintain that they are providing alternatives that will make the landscape a more democratic place in which to live; they emphasize that they are not against everything coming down the tubes.

In addition to meeting the Renaissance Resisters, Allan meets another group of six people for breakfast on alternate Fridays. These people are all administrators whose schools are close to one another and whose students have similar needs. Allan characterizes this group as being full of "contrarian thinkers." This knowledge community also offers Allan a regularly scheduled time to share his narrative knowing:

A: We have good chats and good laughs. . . . It ends the week.
C: It saves you from carrying things home with you over the weekend?
A: Yes. You share what has happened over the week. You have a space to share. . . .

A third group of people, a group of retired principals, form the last of Allan's knowledge community groups. In the following excerpt, he describes the texts that they share and illustrates the mutuality of their relationships:

> Every 2 months I meet with the retirement group of principals. They tell me about . . . their time and freedom. My use to them is that I am their pipeline into what is happening in the school system. They tell me of the afterlife of teaching/principaling.

These people provide Allan with a historical view of the landscape as well as a future guide to life off of it. Allan points to one member of the group, an individual with whom he also meets separately, who particularly helps him gain perspective: "We inform each other. He has cut the string, but he is helpful to me because he has many valuable insights."

Allan repeatedly turns to the people I have just described when he finds himself going against the grain on the landscape. His knowledge communities consistently remind him that alternate thinking reaches back into the human past, plays out in the present, and presses forward into the future. They keep the passion for competing stories alive in him.

Conclusion

In this chapter, I have explored the experiences of Allan, an elementary school principal, on the landscape. I began with an examination of Allan's enactment of his rebel image and unearthed his biography. Next, I explored Allan's knowledge communities and explained how they have supported his expression of his "principal as rebel" image.

Throughout this work, Allan's impulse "to story tell, to be in relationship, and to reflect upon actions taken and things thought" (Clandinin & Connelly, 1995) has prevailed, in spite of, and even because of, the conduit-driven qualities of the landscape he has come to know. By expressing these fundamentally human qualities, Allan has enabled the sacred theory-practice story and the monopoly it has on the landscape to be brought into focus. Furthermore, his enactment of the rebel image has both revealed and validated his personal knowledge and illustrated the challenges he faces in his work as an administrator. But, in spite of the many tensions that Allan and his colleagues have experienced, they have managed to create safe places for themselves off the landscape. These communities of sustenance, these knowledge communities, have served to renew, refresh and ready them to continue their creation and cultivation of competing stories on the landscape.

That people from different places on the landscape are informally coming together to discuss their personal and collective experiences is heartening. Their willingness to entertain other stories of possibility can be heard in the voices of individuals who, like Allan, have found the plotline to the sacred story confining and counterproductive. It seems fitting to end with one of Allan's comments:

> You are [working] at the academic level. . . . We [you and me] cannot do it alone. What it [our collaborative work] will do is encourage others to do the same thing. One wolf crying in the wilderness [is meaningless]. But when you get another wolf answering the first, and a third one answering the first two, and a fourth . . . and when they get together and they start howling together . . . that's when the caribou and the moose get restless.

In Allan's words lie the hope for the professional knowledge landscape—the hope for the future.

PART IV

Reflections on Knowledge, Context, and Identity

In Part IV we reflect on the relationship of knowledge, context, and identity for administrators as we begin to puzzle about how the conduit shapes administrators' identities. The section concludes with comments on how much narrative work needs to be done in understanding administrator knowledge and identity.

CHAPTER 15

Hierarchy and Identity
in the Conduit

As we began this work we realized that institutional stories would strongly influence stories of school on the landscape. We knew these stories to live by would make a difference to teacher identities. Teachers almost always tell their stories as ones in which they are in interaction with what they imagine to be their administrators' stories. And so it was in chapter after chapter.

The administrator stories appear in different guises, sometimes as a depersonalized "they," as, for instance, in Nancy's nursing story; sometimes as a ghostly administrative presence indirectly influencing the teacher's story by hovering over it in judgmental ways as, for instance, in Huber's and Whelan's teaching stories; and sometimes in the embodied, personalized form of an administrator as an integral character in the plotline as, for instance, in Rose's story of his place in Sara's teaching life and in Davies's account of the teachers' response to a new principal's actions. A popular story of teachers and teaching has the teacher in Lone Ranger character roles, doing what they wish, independent of public will and local program implementation directives. Goodlad and Klein's (1970) *Behind the Classroom Door* captured this independent, isolated sense of teaching and helped legitimize that story as the most predominant story of teacher in the professional and scholarly literature. But this is not the portrayal that emerges from the chapters of this book, nor even from our first book on this topic, *Teachers' Professional Knowledge Landscapes*. Quite a different portrayal appears to mark the teachers with whom we worked. They are people with strong teacher identities, identities made up from an amalgam of children, curriculum, beliefs, values, and personal histories. But so too are these identities made up of parents, community, board of education, administration, and administrators.

Teacher identities not only take the form of romantic tales of a "calling," of a most noble profession, of helping the needy. They may also take the form of tales of service, and servant, of doing one's public duty and of obeying, or not, orders from above. There may well be other such tales. Given the idea of a landscape of teaching, these multiple qualities of teacher identity are to be expected. They reflect teachers' positions on the in- and out-of-classroom places on the landscape. What is significant about this way of thinking about teachers and teacher identity is that it reshapes the popular and professional story of teachers, a story that leads everywhere to imagined, often actual, splits between teacher aims, wants, and working conditions and the aims, wants, and working conditions of others on the landscape of teaching.

As we turned to the administrator stories in Part III we hoped to come into direct contact with the "they," the "ghosts," the administrative persons who figure so prominently in teacher identities. Who are these people? What are their identities, their stories to live by? What are their institutional stories, told from their positions, that loom so large in teacher stories to live by?

Casting this simplistically, we might have expected to find administrators embodying the institutional narrative, and the sacred story of transmission via the conduit, in the way that many teacher participants experienced these stories. But what we found was each administrator expressing stories of opposition to the institutional narratives, opposition to the very same kind of directives from above that figure so prominently in each of the teacher stories. Samson is concerned with administrative demands that eat away at her commitment to teachers. Applebaum creates a different form of staff development meeting contrary to the kind she imagines is sanctioned by her board. Allen labels himself a rebel and tells story after story to Craig of his rebellion against almost everything that comes through the conduit to his principal's office.

In her work with school administrators, Marilyn Dickson (1998) found that one of the stories to live by for teachers in transition to administrator involves acquiring the sense of power and influence that accompanies the position. One wonders if her participants, like ours, will chafe at the restrictions on power and influence that life positioned as school administrator appears to entail. We do not know from her participants and can only raise questions for further inquiry. Is professional education, and subsequent life on the landscape, such a dichotomizing force that life from one vantage point on the landscape is misunderstood from another? Do teachers misunderstand issues of power and influence in school administrative positions? What is the understanding of positions in the system higher than that of principal or, as in Applebaum's case, administrator? Is it possible that people think of power and influence as a kind of ever-expanding commodity available in increasing quantities as one moves up an administrative ladder? On this view teachers will understand the limitations of power and influence of administrators immediately above them.

We wonder if we need to change our terms, our way of thinking, about administrator identity. Surprisingly, at least to us, there is little in our administrator stories on which to construct administrator identities, their stories to live by, in the way that we have so far done with teacher identities. Two features figure prominently in the administrator stories of the three preceding chapters. One is the already-named response to directives and information from above them in the conduit. The second is each administrator's reference to teachers whom they administer. In effect, the stories in these chapters are composed of things seen by looking up the conduit, and down to the landscape, from their administrator vantage point. What is missing, perhaps curiously so if viewed from the point of view of the composition of teacher identity, but perhaps not if carefully viewed from an administrator's vantage point, are references to, and stories of, children, curricula, and programs. What appears to be missing are educational stories to live by.

Other than deeper understandings of the pervasiveness of the conduit and of the hierarchy of authority that drives communication through the conduit, we gain little sense of administrator stories to live by. That is, there is little sense of administrator identities that emerge from the stories told. We learn only that administrators seem to choose either a story of conformity to messages in the conduit or rebellion to these messages. However, these stories are instructive to us in what they show us about the conduit.

Hierarchy in the Conduit

The most striking lesson from these three chapters is the hierarchical structure of the conduit. Whereas teachers experience dilemmas moving back and forth between the in- and out-of-classroom places on the landscape, administrators experience dilemmas as they are positioned at the lip of the conduit moving back and forth, even acting simultaneously, between those above them in the conduit—superintendents, trustees—and those who live on the school landscapes with them but who are often described as being below them—teachers and students. We often imagine that when teachers move from the position of teacher to the position of principal they will gain power, influence, and freedom from the power and influence of others. But what these chapters show us is that administrators feel that there is a massive hierarchy above them and that their positions are still those of doing or not doing what is prescribed for them. In this, their dilemmas are no different from those of the teachers.

Grey Ghosts in the Conduit

Allan, the principal in Craig's chapter, uses a metaphor of "grey ghosts" to show how there are people working in institutions who have an intimate understanding of how the conduit works to support the institutional narrative. There is no evidence, no stories, in these chapters to represent this metaphor. But it is helpful in imagining what it is that makes the conduit work when, if our stories are at all indicative, people at different levels resist living out their parts in the institutional story. In effect our account of the landscape is only partial in that we have recorded stories of the resistors, the rebels, but no story of those who might live the part of grey ghosts. Allan's metaphor is particularly insightful—for, after all, how does one learn a ghost story? The description of the transmission and implementation steps in the process of moving ideas and things through the conduit misses the key ghostly figures that keep the conduit functioning.

Individualism and the Conduit

Almost as pervasive as the hierarchy is the sense of individualism that comes through the stories. Allan, again, identifies this in his comment "to thine own self be true." He is arguing that a successful administrator, and he, in particular, needs to be a person with beliefs to stand by in the face of alternate prescriptions from the conduit. There is a strong sense that the individual administrator needs to stand up and be counted. There is also a strong sense in Allan's story that individuals who do this do not get promoted further up the hierarchy.

Allan sees that his standing up for his beliefs in opposition to conduit positions "cost him" in terms of promotion. We wonder if, in Samson's story, this is not one of the messages contained in her principal's advice that she "can't be in administration and teaching too." Perhaps it is her commitment to teachers and her concern about conduit prescriptions taking her away from them that is seen as impossible to her principal. She must choose.

Ideas and the Conduit

If there is one thing that captures the educational in the minds of the public, it is the idea of educational reform. The school system is somehow or another imagined to be a kind of playground for innovation for the public, policy makers, and researchers with new and ingenious ideas. But what appears in the stories we have, and what might appear to be the case more generally, is that innovation, new ideas, must be sanctioned by the existing ideology of the conduit. Allan makes this point when he says, "I was not in the ideology" that would have allowed him to advance an innovative idea of an ideal school. He imagines that one needs to be a grey ghost to bring about an innovation. We, however, think he has not taken his point as far as he might. In effect, prevailing ideology defines what an innovation may be. Not even grey ghosts would be able to introduce an idea that did not fit with the ideology. Indeed, the prevailing ideology is more or less defined by the network of such grey ghosts. We see something similar in Applebaum's experiment with democratic decision making on a professional-development day. She sees this approach to professional development as falling outside the prevailing ideology. Although she conducts an innovative experiment with her staff, she also anticipates that the staff meeting might not accomplish the institutional mandates. In order to still fit within the ideology, she prepares, and eventually distributes, a document that meets conduit requirements.

Conclusion

As we reflected on these stories, we realized we have, in effect, returned to our starting point with a description of the sacred story that connects theory to practice. Although our understanding of the conduit is now more complex, we realize that we still have not heard administrators' stories to live by. We do not have the material to discuss administrators' identities, their stories to live by, except insofar as their stories are told in relation to the conduit. We wonder at this gap. Why is it that the teacher stories are so rich in terms of issues of identity and the administrator stories so silent on this matter? Is it because the only stories they can live are those of hierarchy and of various degrees of conformity and resistance to the conduit? From this possible way of looking at the question, the sacred theory/practice story and all it entails is so pervasive as to be inescapable. It means, if we follow this line of thinking, that there is no place on the landscape of schooling for genuine alternatives. This line of thinking opens up a new line of questions for us. If the conduit is so pervasive as to fix administrator identities, how might we imagine a system that created possibilities for alternatives and, therefore, possibilities for the formation of different identities?

John Dewey argued that social reconstruction came about through inquiry into the conditions of social life. But even inquiry needs to be sanctioned. It, too, is an idea. Somehow pockets of spaces for alternatives need to find a home on the landscape. They need to be places where administrators and others can work together in ways that do not place them within a hierarchy, ways in which the "natural" tendency is not to look up and down but for us to look to one another for sources of ideas, sources of authority, and sources of action.

References

Bateson, M. C. (1994). *Peripheral visions: Learning along the way.* New York: HarperCollins.

Bergsma, J. (Painter). (1983). Bergsma collectibles [Print]. Bellingham, WA: Available from Jody Bergsma Galleries, Inc.

Clandinin, D. J., & Connelly, F. M. (1995). *Teachers' professional knowledge landscapes.* New York: Teachers College Press.

Clandinin, D. J., & Connelly, F. M. (1996). Teachers' professional knowledge landscapes: Teacher stories—stories of teachers—school stories—stories of schools. *Educational Researcher, 25*(3), 24–30.

Clark, C. M., & Peterson, P. L. (1986). Teachers' thought processes. In M. C. Wittrock (Ed.), *Handbook of research on teaching* (pp. 255–296). New York: Macmillan.

Connelly, F. M., & Clandinin, D. J. (1988). *Teachers as curriculum planners: Narratives of experience.* New York: Teachers College Press.

Connelly, F. M., & Clandinin, D. J. (1990a). The cyclic temporal structure of schooling. In M. Ben Peretz & R. Bromme (Eds.), *The nature of time in schools: Theoretical concepts, practitioner perceptions* (pp. 36–63). New York: Teachers College Press.

Connelly, F. M., & Clandinin, D. J. (1990b). Stories of experience and narrative inquiry. *Educational Researcher, 19*(5), 2–14.

Connelly, F. M., & Clandinin, D. J. (1993). Cycles, rhythms, and the meaning of school time. In L. W. Anderson & H. J. Walberg (Eds.), *Timepiece: Extending and enhancing learning time* (pp. 9–14). Reston, VA: National Association of Secondary School Principals.

Crites, S. (1971). The narrative quality of experience. *Journal of the American Academy of Religion, 399*(3), 291–311.

Dewey, J. (1938). *Experience and education.* New York: Collier Books.

Dickson, M. (1998, June). *Slipping the bonds: A narrative inquiry of elementary women educators in leadership roles.* Unpublished doctoral dissertation, University of Toronto.

Feiman-Nemser, S., & Floden, R. E. (1986). The cultures of teaching. In M. C. Wittrock (Ed.), *Handbook of research on teaching* (pp. 505–526). New York: Macmillan.

Gauthier, D. P. (1963). *Practical reasoning.* Oxford: Clarendon Press.

Geertz, C. (1995). *After the fact: Two countries, four decades, one anthropologist.* Cambridge, MA: Harvard University Press.

Gilligan, C. (1982). *In a different voice: Psychological theory and women's development*. Cambridge, MA: Harvard University Press.

Goodlad, J. I., & Klein, M. (1970). *Behind the classroom door*. Worthington, OH: Jones.

He, Ming Fang. (1995, August). A cross-cultural perspective on the impact of metaphors on teachers' thinking. Paper presented at the meeting of the International Association on Teachers' Thinking.

Johnson, M. (1987). *The body in the mind: The bodily basis of meaning, imagination, and reason*. Chicago: University of Chicago Press.

Krueger, L. (1995, November 24). The case for urging older profs to retire. *The Globe and Mail*, p. A22.

Landry, C. (1976). Hi God [Cassette Recording]. Phoenix: North American Liturgy.

Lane, B. (1988). *Landscapes of the sacred: Geography and narrative in American spirituality*. New York: Paulist Press.

Lionni, L. (1963). *Swimmy*. New York: Knopf.

Mazer, A. (1991). *The salamander room*. New York: Knopf.

Metzger, D. (1992). *Writing for your life: A guide and companion to the inner worlds*. San Francisco: HarperCollins.

Mills, L. (1991). *The rag coat*. Toronto: Little, Brown.

Phillion, J. (1995). Field texts. Teachers' professional knowledge landscapes in transition. Social Sciences and Humanities Research Council of Canada, F. M. Connelly & D. J. Clandinin.

Polanyi, M. (1958). *Personal knowledge: Towards a post-critical philosophy*. Chicago: University of Chicago Press.

Renner, K. E. (1995). *The new agenda for higher education*. Calgary: Detselig Enterprises.

Schön, D. A. (1983). *The reflective practitioner: How professionals think in action*. New York: Basic Books.

Schön, D. A. (1991). *The reflective turn: Case studies in and on educational practice*. New York: Teachers College Press.

Schwab, J. J. (1970). *The practical: A language for curriculum*. Washington, DC: National Education Association, Center for the Study of Instruction. [Reprinted in Westbury & Wilkoff, *Science, curriculum, and liberal education: Selected essays*. Chicago: University of Chicago Press. 1978.]

Soltis, J. F. (1995). Foreword. In D. J. Clandinin & F. M. Connelly, *Teachers' Professional Knowledge Landscapes* (pp. vii–viii). New York: Teachers College Press.

Stevenson, S. (1989). *Learning to live new rhythms of teaching*. Unpublished master's project, University of Calgary.

Untermeyer, L. (1956). *The road not taken: An introduction to Robert Frost*. New York: Holt, Rinehart, and Winston.

Van Maanen, J. (1988). *Tales of the field: On writing ethnography*. Chicago: University of Chicago Press.

Wittrock, M. C. (Ed.). (1986). *Handbook of research on teaching* (3rd ed.). A Project of the American Educational Research Association. New York: Macmillan.

Yashima, T. (1955). *Crow boy*. New York: Puffin Books.

Index

About the Contributors

F. Michael Connelly studied at the University of Alberta, Columbia University, and at the University of Chicago. He is professor and Director, Joint Centre for Teacher Development, Ontario Institute for Studies in Education and the Faculty of Education, University of Toronto. He taught secondary school in Alberta and held teaching positions at the Universities of Alberta, Illinois, and Chicago. He coordinated the Canadian component of the Second International Science Study, is editor of *Curriculum Inquiry*, and is a former member of the board of directors of the John Dewey Society for Study of Education and Culture. He is co-director, with D. Jean Clandinin, of a long-term study of teachers' personal practical knowledge and teachers' professional knowledge landscapes. Drs. Connelly and Clandinin are co-authors of *Teachers as Curriculum Planners: Narratives of Experience* (1988), as well as numerous articles and chapters in contributed volumes. Dr. Connelly was the recipient of the 1987 Outstanding Canadian Curriculum Scholar Award of the Canadian Society for the Study of Education and the 1991 Canadian Education Association/Whitworth award for Educational Research.

D. Jean Clandinin is a former teacher, counselor, and school psychologist. She obtained her B.A. and M.Ed. from the University of Alberta and her Ph.D. from the University of Toronto. She worked at the Ontario Institute for Studies in Education, the University of Calgary, and the University of Alberta. She is currently a professor and Director of the Centre for Research for Teacher Education and Development at the University of Alberta. She has co-authored many books and articles and values her collaborative research with colleagues in schools and universities.

Sheila Dermer Applebaum is an administrator at the Toronto District School Board where she has played a fundamental role in developing programs and teaching materials for adult English as a second language, literacy, and native languages. In 1998 she received her Doctor of Education from the University of Toronto with her thesis, "Conversations in Counterpoint: A Narrative Inquiry into the Professional Knowledge Landscape of Female Administrators at a Board of Education."

Norman Beach teaches Adult ESL for the Toronto District School Board and presents seminars on educational topics including teaching developing country issues and the influence of media on lives. He is the co-author of the book *A Glimpse Behind the Scene: Six ESL Lessons* (1995).

Formerly a Social Sciences and Humanities Research Council of Canada Doctoral and Post-Doctoral Fellow, **Cheryl Craig** is on faculty at Rice University, Houston, Texas and is Senior Researcher in the Center for Education. Her current research is situated at the interstices where principal knowledge, teacher knowledge, school context, and school reform meet. Inquiry, collaboration, and community are central features of Craig's work.

Annie Davies received her initial teacher training in Birmingham, England, and has been an elementary school teacher in Alberta for the past thirty years. She completed her Ph.D. in Teacher Education in 1996 at the University of Alberta and continues to enjoy her involvement in collaborative research projects, nurtured by the direction of Jean and Michael, which allow opportunities for publication.

Jinjiang Du holds Master's Degrees in linguistics and applied linguistics from China and Great Britain. Specializing in teaching English as a Second/Foreign Language, he taught in Xinjiang University and Guangzhou Institute of Foreign Languages in China before emigrating to Canada. His Ph.D. with OISE was completed except for his dissertation. He has been working with the Toronto District School Board since 1990.

Ming Fang He was educated in Wuhan University of Hydraulic and Electrical Engineering, China, Lakehead University and OISE/UT, Canada. She received her Doctorate at the Centre for Teacher Development at OISE/UT under the supervision of Michael Connelly. Her research was a cross-cultural study of identity development in Chinese women teachers as they moved back and forth between Chinese and Canadian cultures.

Janice Huber is an elementary teacher who has worked in rural, urban, and international school contexts with children of diverse backgrounds. Her participation in ongoing collaborating inquiry groups, made possible through Jean and Michael's work on teacher knowledge and professional landscapes, has been a place of sustained inquiry central to her evolving practice as a teacher, and her current work as a doctoral candidate at The Centre for Research for Teacher Education and Development.

JoAnn Phillion taught English as a Second Language in Japan for six years. After returning to Canada, she taught immigrant students. She is a Ph.D. candidate at the Centre for Teacher Development at OISE/ University of Toronto. In her research she focuses on an immigrant teacher's experiences in an inner-city, community school.

Sally Quan is a Nursing Professor at George Brown Community College in Toronto. She is a doctoral candidate in Education at the Ontario Institute for Studies in Education, University of Toronto, studying the field of curriculum. She has co-authored a number of reports and publications in the fields of nursing, curriculum, and equity.

After 33 years in public education, **Chuck Rose** is currently an educational consultant, research associate, and professor. He began teaching in 1963, became a principal in 1970 and worked in elementary, elementary-junior high, junior high, and central office settings. He received an M.A. from the University of Calgary in 1989 and Ph.D. from the University of Alberta in 1997.

Florence Samson is completing her doctoral dissertation under the supervision of Michael Connelly, Centre for Teacher Development. Florence, mother of two sons and a daughter, is a teacher/administrator. Her research focus is the split/dilemma/conflict which women experience as they integrate family and career. She has co-authored teacher induction and common curriculum documents for use in the Atlantic Provinces.

Karen Whelan has taught with Edmonton Public Schools over the past eight years in both elementary and junior high settings, with experiences across a wide range of cultural backgrounds and socio-economic contexts. Her desire to explore the stories which emerged from various school landscapes became possible in relationship with multiple inquiry groups, nurtured through Jean and Michael's ongoing narrative research into teaching and teacher education. Karen continues her relational research story alongside Janice, as she is currently working on her doctoral program